William C Hoff

Hymns of Praise and Patriotism

William C Hoff

Hymns of Praise and Patriotism

ISBN/EAN: 9783337309466

Printed in Europe, USA, Canada, Australia, Japan

Cover: Foto ©Thomas Meinert / pixelio.de

More available books at **www.hansebooks.com**

Hymns of Praise & Patriotism

SELECTED AND ARRANGED
BY WILLIAM C. HOFF, SUPER-
VISOR OF MUSIC IN THE PUBLIC
SCHOOLS OF YONKERS, N. Y.

TOWNSEND MacCOUN
NEW YORK   MDCCCXCVII

Author's Preface

THE object of the compiler of this book has been to select a number of the best standard hymns, national and patriotic songs, for use in the public schools, together with a few psalms for responsive reading, arranged and pointed for chanting if so desired. They are unsectarian in their character and can be used by persons of any denomination.

The tune names of hymns are given and they may be found in any hymnal in common use.

The music of most of the national patriotic selections may be found in "Songs of the Nation," published by Silver, Burdett & Company.

The compiler gratefully acknowledges the courtesies extended to him by Messrs. Oliver Ditson & Co., Biglow & Main, Novello, Ewer & Co., Houghton Mifflin & Co., E. P. Dutton & Co., A. D. F. Randolph & Co., Dr. J. E. Rankin, Thomas S. Hastings, Charles S. Robinson, P. Prentice, G. Putnam, and H. H. Duffield.

WILLIAM C. HOFF.

YONKERS, July 15, 1897.

Publisher's Preface

This book is made primarily for such Public Schools as have singing in their general exercises. To such schools the question of supplying each pupil with a hymn book or book of patriotic songs is one of cost. Though sight reading in music may be taught in the school, yet, as a matter of fact, three-fourths of the scholars in any school, do not, and never will, sing by note in general exercises. A copy, therefore, of any standard hymnal with music, for use at the instrument, and inexpensive copies of the words for each pupil, best meet all the requirements at a minimum of cost.

To supply such a book for the pupils is the object of this collection.

The same principle applies, and the book is equally well adapted for use in Sabbath-Schools and Churches.

TOWNSEND MACCOUN.

NEW YORK, July 15, 1897.

Order of Arrangement

Hymns for Special Occasions:

                                                              HYMNS

    Morning and Evening, ... 1–16

    Christmas, ... 17–24

    Thanksgiving, ... 25–26

    New Year, ... 27–28

    Easter, ... 29–32

General Selections, ... 33–134

Chants, ... 135–149

Patriotic Selections, ... 150–163

Index of First Lines, . . . *Pages* 184–187

Hymns

For Special Occasions

Regent Square. 8s. and 7s.

Key of C. First Note—5. H. Smart.

1

GRACIOUS God, our Heavenly Father!
　Meet and bless our school, we pray;
As in humble trust we gather,
　Teachers, scholars, here to-day.
Every joy and every blessing
　From Thy bounteous hand we own;
May Thy love, our souls possessing,
　Draw us nearer to Thy throne.

2 Weak, imperfect, tempted, erring,
　From Thy precepts, Lord, we stray;
Let Thy Spirit, from our wandering,
　Bring us back to virtue's way.
Humble, penitent, confiding,
　May we rest our hope in Thee;
In Thy favor, Lord, abiding,
　In Thy peace and purity.

UNKNOWN.

Morning Hymn. L. M.

Key of A. First Note—1. F. H. Bartholemon.

2

AWAKE, my soul, and with the sun
　Thy daily stage of duty run;
Shake off dull sloth, and early rise
To pay thy morning sacrifice.

2 Redeem thy misspent time that's past,
　And live this day as if thy last;
Improve thy talent with due care;
For the great Day thyself prepare.

THOMAS KEN.

Halle. 7. 6.

Key of G.   First Note—1.   F. J. Haydn.

3

EVERY morning mercies new
    Fall as fresh as morning dew;
Every morning let us pay
Tribute with the early day;
For Thy mercies, Lord, are sure;
Thy compassion doth endure.

2 Still the greatness of Thy love
Daily doth our sins remove;
Daily, far as east from west,
Lifts the burden from the breast;
Gives unbought to those who pray
Strength to stand in evil day.

3 Let our prayers each morn prevail,
That these gifts may never fail;
And, as we confess the sin
And the tempter's power within,
Feed us with the Bread of Life;
Fit us for our daily strife.

4 As the morning light returns,
As the sun with splendor burns,
Teach us still to turn to Thee,
Ever blessed Trinity,
With our hands our hearts to raise,
In unfailing prayer and praise.

H. BONAR.

Warwick. C. M.

Key of E♭. First Note—1. S. Stanley.

4

ONCE more, my soul, the rising day
  Salutes thy waking eyes;
Once more, my voice, thy tribute pay
  To Him that rules the skies.

2 Night unto night His Name repeats,
  The day renews the sound;
Wide as the heaven on which He sits,
  To turn the seasons round.

3 'Tis He supports my mortal frame;
  My tongue shall speak His praise;
My sins would rouse His wrath to flame;
  And yet His wrath delays.

4 A thousand wretched souls are fled
  Since the last setting sun;
And yet Thou lengthenest out my thread,
  And yet my moments run.

5 Dear God, let all my hours be Thine,
  While I enjoy the light:
Then shall my sun in smiles decline,
  And bring a pleasant night.

I. WATTS.

Forsaken. 11s.

Key of G. First Note—5.   Koschat.

5

THE Lord is my Shepherd, how happy am I!
  How tender and watchful my wants to sup-
    ply!
He daily provides me with raiment and food,
Whate'er He denies me is meant for my good.

2 The Lord is my Shepherd, how happy am I!
I'm blest while I live, and I'm blest when I die:
In death's gloomy valley no evil I'll dread,
For "I will be with Thee," my Shepherd hath
    said.

3 The Lord is my Shepherd, I'll sing with delight,
Till called to adore Him in regions of light:
Then praise Him, with angels, to bright harps of
    gold,
And ever and ever His glory behold.

                               JAMES MONTGOMERY.

Eventide. 10s.

Key of E♭.   First Note—3.   W. H. Monk.

6

ABIDE with me: fast falls the eventide;
 The darkness deepens; Lord, with me abide:
When other helpers fail, and comforts flee,
Help of the helpless, oh, abide with me.

2 Swift to its close ebbs out life's little day;
Earth's joys grow dim, its glories pass away,
Change and decay in all around I see;
O Thou Who changest not, abide with me.

3 I need Thy presence every passing hour;
What but Thy grace can foil the tempter's power!
Who, like Thyself, my guide and stay can be?
Through cloud and sunshine, Lord, abide with me.

H. F. LYTE.

St. Leonard. C. M.

KEY OF G.   FIRST NOTE—1.   H. SMART.

7

1. THE shadows of the evening hours
    Fall from the darkening sky;
   Upon the fragrance of the flowers
    The dews of evening lie.

2. Before Thy throne, O Lord of heaven
    We kneel at close of day;
   Look on Thy children from on high,
    And hear us while we pray.

3. The sorrows of Thy servants, Lord,
    Oh, do not Thou despise,
   But let the incense of our prayers
    Before Thy mercy rise.

4. The brightness of the coming night
    Upon the darkness rolls;
   With hopes of future glory chase
    The shadows on our souls.

5. Slowly the rays of daylight fade:
    So fade within our heart
   The hopes in earthly love and joy,
    That one by one depart.

6. Slowly the bright stars, one by one,
    Within the heavens shine:
   Give us, O Lord, fresh hopes in heaven,
    And trust in things divine.

                          ADELAIDE A. PROCTER.

Merrial. 6. 5.

Key of A. First Note—5.   J. Barnby

8

NOW the day is over,
  Night is drawing nigh;
Shadows of the evening
  Steal across the sky;

2 Jesus, give the weary
    Calm and sweet repose;
  With Thy tenderest blessing
    May our eyelids close.

3 Grant to little children
    Visions bright of Thee;
  Guard the sailors tossing
    On the deep, blue sea.

4 Comfort every sufferer
    Watching late in pain;
  Those who plan some evil
    From their sins restrain.

5 Through the long night-watches,
    May Thine angels spread
  Their white wings above me,
    Watching round my bed.

6 When the morning wakens,
    Then may I arise
  Pure, and fresh, and sinless
    In Thy holy eyes.

S. BARING GOULD.

Chesterfield. C. M.

Key of G. First Note—5.   T. Haweis.

9

SHINE on our souls, eternal God,
  With rays of beauty shine;
Oh let Thy favor crown our days,
  And all their round be Thine.

2 With Thee let every week begin,
   With Thee each day be spent,
 For Thee each fleeting hour employed,
   Since each by Thee is lent.

3 Thus cheer us through this desert road,
   Till all our labors cease;
 And heaven refresh our weary souls
   With everlasting peace.

                    PHILIP DODDRIDGE.

Thursley. L. M.

Key of F. First Note—1.   W. H. Monk.

10

SUN of my soul, Thou Saviour dear,
It is not night if Thou be near;
Oh, may no earth-born cloud arise
To hide Thee from Thy servant's eyes.

2 When the soft dews of kindly sleep
My weary eyelids gently steep,
Be my last thought, how sweet to rest
Forever on my Saviour's breast.

3 Abide with me from morn till eve,
For without Thee I cannot live;
Abide with me when night is nigh,
For without Thee I dare not die.

4 If some poor wandering child of Thine
Have spurned to-day the voice divine,
Now, Lord, the gracious work begin;
Let him no more lie down in sin.

J. KEBLE.

Weber. 7s.

KEY OF F. FIRST NOTE—3.   FROM VON WEBER.

11

SOFTLY now the light of day
  Fades upon my sight away;
Free from care, from labor free,
Lord, I would commune with Thee.

2 Thou, Whose all-pervading eye
    Naught escapes, without, within,
  Pardon each infirmity,
    Open fault, and secret sin.

3 Soon, for me, the light of day
  Shall forever pass away;
  Then, from sin and sorrow free,
  Take me, Lord, to dwell with Thee.

4 Thou Who, sinless, yet hast known
    All of man's infirmity;
  Then, from Thine eternal throne,
    Jesus, look with pitying eye.

                                G. W. DOANE.

Tallis's Hymn. L. M.

Key of G.   First Note—1.   T. Tallis.

12

All praise to Thee, my God, this night,
For all the blessings of the light;
Keep me, Oh, keep me, King of kings,
Beneath Thine own almighty wings.

2 Forgive me, Lord, for Thy dear Son,
The ill that I this day have done;
That with the world, myself, and Thee,
I, ere I sleep, at peace may be.

3 Teach me to live, that I may dread
The grave as little as my bed;
Teach me to die, that so I may
Rise glorious at the awful day.

4 Oh, may my soul on Thee repose,
And may sweet sleep mine eyelids close;
Sleep that shall me more vigorous make
To serve my God when I awake.

T. Ken.

Belmont. C. M.

Key of G.   First Note—1.   S. Webbe.

13

Now from the altar of our hearts
   Let flames of love arise;
Assist us, Lord, to offer up
   Our evening sacrifice.

2 Minutes and mercies multiplied
   Have made up all this day;
Minutes came quick, but mercies were
   More swift, more free than they.

3 New time, new favors, and new joys
   Do a new song require;
Till we shall praise Thee as we would,
   Accept our hearts' desire.

J. MASON.

Ellerton. 10s.

Key of A♭. First Note—5. E. J. Hopkins.

14

SAVIOUR, again to Thy dear Name we raise
  With one accord our parting hymn of praise;
We stand to bless Thee ere our worship cease,
Then, lowly kneeling, wait Thy word of peace.

2 Grant us Thy peace through this approaching night,
  Turn Thou for us its darkness into light;
  From harm and danger keep Thy children free,
  For dark and light are both alike to Thee.

3 Grant us Thy peace upon our homeward way;
  With Thee began, with Thee shall end the day;
  Guard Thou the lips from sin, the hearts from shame,
  That in this house have called upon Thy Name.

J. ELLERTON.

Fernshaw. C. M.

Key of G. First Note—5.   J. Booth.

15

BLEST day of God! most calm, most bright,
 The first, the best of days;
The laborer's rest, the saint's delight,
 The day of prayer and praise.

2 My Saviour's face made thee to shine;
 His rising thee did raise,
And made thee heavenly and divine
 Beyond all other days.

3 The first-fruits oft a blessing prove
 To all the sheaves behind;
And they the day of Christ who love,
 A happy week shall find.

4 This day I must with God appear;
 For, Lord, the day is Thine;
Help me to spend it in Thy fear,
 And thus to make it mine.

J. MASON.

Dies Dominica. 7. 6.

Key of E. First Note—3. J. B. Dykes.

16

O DAY of rest and gladness,
   O day of joy and light,
O balm of care and sadness,
   Most beautiful, most bright;
On thee, the high and lowly,
   Through ages joined in tune,
Sing, Holy, Holy, Holy,
   To the great God Triune.

2 On thee, at the creation,
   The light first had its birth;
On thee for our salvation
   Christ rose from depths of earth;
On thee our Lord victorious
   The Spirit sent from heaven;
And thus on thee most glorious
   A triple light was given.

3 Thou art a port protected
   From storms that round us rise;
A garden intersected
   With streams of Paradise;
Thou art a cooling fountain
   In life's dry, dreary sand;
From thee, like Pisgah's mountain,
   We view our promised land.

4 To-day on weary nations
   The heavenly manna falls:
To holy convocations
   The silver trumpet calls,
Where Gospel light is glowing
   With pure and radiant beams,
And living water flowing
   With soul-refreshing streams.

C. WORDSWORTH.

Adeste Fideles. P. M.

KEY OF A. FIRST NOTE—1.   J. READING.

17

OH COME, all ye faithful, joyful and triumphant;
Oh come ye, oh come ye to Bethlehem;
  Come and behold Him born the King of angels;
Oh come, let us adore Him,
Oh come, let us adore Him,
Oh come, let us adore Him, Christ the Lord.

2   Sing, choirs of angels, sing in exultation,
  Sing, all ye citizens of heaven above,
    Glory to God in the highest;
  Oh come, let us adore Him, etc.

3   Yea, Lord, we greet Thee, born this happy morning;
  Jesu, to Thee be glory given;
    Word of the Father, now in flesh appearing;
  Oh come, let us adore Him,
  Oh come, let us adore Him,
  Oh come, let us adore Him, Christ the Lord.

TRANSLATED BY F. OAKELEY.

Herald Angels. 7s.

KEY OF G. FIRST NOTE—5.   MENDELSSOHN.

18

HARK! the herald angels sing
  Glory to the new-born King;
Peace on earth, and mercy mild,
God and sinners reconciled!

2 Joyful, all ye nations, rise,
  Join the triumph of the skies;
With the angelic host proclaim,
Christ is born in Bethlehem!

3 Veiled in flesh the Godhead see;
Hail the Incarnate Deity,
Pleased as Man with man to dwell;
Jesus, our Emmanuel!

4 Mild He lays His glory by,
Born that man no more may die,
Born to raise the sons of earth,
Born to give them second birth.

5 Risen with healing in His wings,
Light and life to all He brings,-
Hail, the Sun of Righteousness!
Hail, the heaven-born Prince of Peace!

                     CHARLES WESLEY.

Gabriel. C. M.

Key of C.   First Note—5.   Traditional.

19

WHILE shepherds watched their flocks by night,
   All seated on the ground,
The angel of the Lord came down,
   And glory shone around.

2 "Fear not," said he, for mighty dread
   Had seized their troubled mind;
"Glad tidings of great joy I bring
   To you and all mankind.

3 "To you, in David's town, this day
   Is born of David's line,
The Saviour, Who is Christ the Lord;
   And this shall be the sign:

4 "The heavenly Babe you there shall find
   To human view displayed;
All meanly wrapt in swathing bands,
   And in a manger laid."

5 Thus spake the seraph; and forthwith
   Appeared a shining throng
Of angels praising God, who thus
   Addressed their joyful song.

N. TATE.

Carol. D. C. M.

Key of B♭. First Note—5. R. S. Willis.

20

It came upon the midnight clear,
  That glorious song of old,
From angels bending near the earth
  To touch their harps of gold;
Peace on the earth, good-will to men,
  From heaven's all-gracious King;
The world in solemn stillness lay
  To hear the angels sing.

2 Still through the cloven skies they come,
  With peaceful wings unfurled;
And still their heavenly music floats
  O'er all the weary world:
Above its sad and lonely plains
  They bend on hovering wing,
And ever o'er its Babel sounds
  The blessèd angels sing.

3 O ye, beneath life's crushing load,
  Whose forms are bending low,
Who toil along the climbing way
  With painful steps and slow!
Look now, for glad and golden hours
  Come swiftly on the wing:
Oh, rest beside the weary road,
  And hear the angels sing.

4 For lo, the days are hastening on,
  By prophets seen of old,
When with the ever-circling years,
  Shall come the time foretold,
When the new heaven and earth shall own
  The Prince of Peace their King,
And the whole world send back the song
  Which now the angels sing.

E. H. Sears.

Aveson. P. M.

Key of F. First Note—5.

21

SHOUT the glad tidings, exultingly sing,
 Jerusalem triumphs, Messiah is king.

1 Sion, the marvellous story be telling,
   The Son of the Highest, how lowly His birth!
 The brightest archangel in glory excelling,
   He stoops to redeem thee, He reigns upon earth.

Shout the glad tidings, etc.

2 Tell how He cometh; from nation to nation
   The heart-cheering news let the earth echo round:
 How free to the faithful He offers salvation,
   How His people with joy everlasting are crowned:

Shout the glad tidings, etc.

3 Mortals, your homage be gratefully bringing,
   And sweet let the gladsome hosanna arise:
 Ye angels, the full alleluia be singing;
   One chorus resound through the earth and the skies:

Shout the glad tidings, etc.

W. A. MUHLENBERG.

St. Louis. P. M.

KEY OF G. FIRST NOTE—3.   L. H. REDNER.

22

O LITTLE town of Bethlehem!
  How still we see thee lie;
Above thy deep and dreamless sleep
  The silent stars go by;
Yet in thy dark streets shineth
  The everlasting Light;
The hopes and fears of all the years
  Are met in thee to-night.

2 For Christ is born of Mary,
    And gathered all above,
  While mortals sleep, the angels keep
    Their watch of wondering love.
  O morning stars, together
    Proclaim the holy birth!
  And praises sing to God the King
    And peace to men on earth.

3 How silently, how silently,
    The wondrous gift is given!
  So God imparts to human hearts
    The blessings of His heaven.
  No ear may hear His coming,
    But in this world of sin,
  Where meek souls will receive Him still,
    The dear Christ enters in.

4 O holy Child of Bethlehem!
    Descend to us, we pray;
  Cast out our sin, and enter in,
    Be born in us to-day.
  We hear the Christmas angels
    The great glad tidings tell;
  Oh come to us, abide with us,
    Our Lord Emmanuel!

By permission of E. P. Dutton & Co.   PHILLIPS-BROOKS.

Regent Square. 8. 7. 8. 7. 4. 7.

KEY OF C.   FIRST NOTE—5.   H. SMART.

23

ANGELS, from the realms of glory,
 Wing your flight o'er all the earth;
Ye, who sang creation's story,
 Now proclaim Messiah's birth:
  Come and worship,
 Worship Christ, the new-born King.

2 Shepherds in the field abiding,
 Watching o'er your flocks by night;
God with man is now residing,
 Yonder shines the infant-light:
  Come and worship,
 Worship Christ, the new-born King.

3 Sages, leave your contemplations;
 Brighter visions beam afar:
Seek the great Desire of nations,
 Ye have seen His natal star:
  Come and worship,
 Worship Christ, the new-born King.

4 Saints before the altar bending,
 Watching long in hope and fear,
Suddenly the Lord, descending,
 In His temple shall appear:
  Come and worship,
 Worship Christ, the new-born King.

JAMES MONTGOMERY.

Nativity. C. M.

Key of B♭.   First Note—3.   H. Lahee.

24

JOY to the world! the Lord is come:
   Let earth receive her King;
Let every heart prepare Him room,
   And heaven and nature sing.

2 Joy to the world! the Saviour reigns:
   Let men their songs employ;
While fields and floods, rocks, hills and plains,
   Repeat the sounding joy.

3 No more let sins and sorrows grow,
   Nor thorns infest the ground;
He comes to make His blessings flow
   Far as the curse is found.

4 He rules the world with truth and grace,
   And makes the nations prove
The glories of His righteousness,
   And wonders of His love.

                           I. Watts.

Dix. 7s.

Key of A. First Note—1.　　　　　　　C Kocher.

25

PRAISE to God, immortal praise,
　For the love that crowns our days;
Bounteous source of every joy,
Let Thy praise our tongues employ;
All to Thee, our God, we owe,
Source whence all our blessings flow.

2 All the plenty summer pours;
Autumn's rich o'erflowing stores;
Flocks that whiten all the plain;
Yellow sheaves of ripened grain:
Lord, for these our souls shall raise
Grateful vows and solemn praise.

3 Peace, prosperity, and health,
Private bliss, and public wealth,
Knowledge with its gladdening streams,
Pure religion's holier beams:
Lord, for these our souls shall raise
Grateful vows and solemn praise.

4 As Thy prospering hand hath blest,
May we give Thee of our best;
And by deeds of kindly love
For Thy mercies grateful prove;
Singing thus through all our days,
Praise to God, immortal praise.

　　　　　　　　　　　L. Barbauld.

St. George or Windsor. 7s.

Key of G. First Note—3. G. J. Elvey.

26

COME, ye thankful people, come,
Raise the song of harvest-home:
All is safely gathered in,
Ere the winter storms begin:
God, our Maker, doth provide
For our wants to be supplied;
Come to God's own temple, come,
Raise the song of harvest-home.

2 All the world is God's own field,
Fruit unto His praise to yield;
Wheat and tares together sown,
Unto joy or sorrow grown:
First the blade, and then the ear,
Then the full corn shall appear:
Grant, O harvest Lord, that we
Wholesome grain and pure may be.

3 For the Lord our God shall come,
And shall take His harvest home;
From His field shall in that day
All offences purge away;
Give His angels charge at last
In the fire the tares to cast,
But the fruitful ears to store
In His garner evermore.

4 Even so, Lord, quickly come
To Thy final harvest-home;
Gather Thou Thy people in,
Free from sorrow, free from sin;
There, forever purified,
In Thy presence to abide:
Come, with all Thine angels, come,
Raise the glorious harvest-home.

HENRY ALFORD.

Berthold. 7. 6.

Key of E♭. First Note—3.   B. Tours.

27

From glory unto glory! Be this our joyous song;
As on the King's own highway, we bravely march along.
From glory unto glory! O word of stirring cheer,
As dawns the solemn brightness of another glad New Year.

2 From glory unto glory! What great things He hath done,
What wonders He hath shown us, what triumphs He hath won!
From glory unto glory! What mighty blessings crown
The lives for which our Lord hath laid His own so freely down!

3 The fulness of His blessing encompasseth our way;
The fulness of His promises crowns every brightening day;
The fulness of His glory is beaming from above,
While more and more we learn to know the fulness of His love.

4 Now onward, ever onward, from strength to strength we go,
While grace for grace abundantly shall from His fulness flow,
To glory's full fruition, from glory's foretaste here,
Until His very presence crown our happiest New Year.

F. R. Havergal.

Benevento. 7s. d.

KEY OF F.   FIRST NOTE—1.   S. WEBBE.

28

WHILE with ceaseless course the sun
  Hasteth through the former year,
Many souls their race have run
  Never-more to meet us here;
Fixed in an eternal state
  They have done with all below;
We a little longer wait,
  But how little none can know.

2 As the winged arrow flies
  Speedily the mark to find;
As the lightning from the skies
  Darts, and leaves no trace behind;
Swiftly thus our fleeting days
  Bear us down life's rapid stream;
Upward, Lord, our spirits raise,
  All below is but a dream.

3 Thanks for mercies past receive;
  Pardon of our sins renew;
Teach us henceforth how to live
  With eternity in view:
Bless Thy word to young and old;
  Fill us with a Saviour's love;
And when life's short tale is told,
  May we dwell with Thee above.
                              JOHN NEWTON.

Easter Hymn. 7s.

KEY OF C. FIRST NOTE—5. W. H. MONK.

29

JESUS Christ is risen to-day,
 Our triumphant holy day,
Who did once upon the cross
Suffer to redeem our loss.
    Alleluia!

2 Hymns of praise then let us sing
 Unto Christ, our heavenly king,
Who endured the cross and grave,
Sinners to redeem and save.
    Alleluia!

3 But the pains which He endured,
 Our salvation have procured;
Now above the sky He's King,
Where the angels ever sing
    Alleluia!

4 Sing we to our God above
 Praise eternal as His love;
Praise Him, all ye heavenly host,
Father, Son, and Holy Ghost;
    Alleluia!

ANON.

St. George, or Windsor. 7s.

Key of G.   First Note—3.   G. J. Elvey.

30

AT the Lamb's high feast we sing
   Praise to our victorious King,
Who hath washed us in the tide
Flowing from His piercèd side;
Praise we Him, Whose love divine
Gives His sacred blood for wine,
Gives His body for the feast,
Christ the victim, Christ the priest.

2 Where the Paschal blood is poured,
   Death's dark angel sheathes his sword;
   Israel's hosts triumphant go
   Through the wave that drowns the foe.
   Praise we Christ, Whose blood was shed,
   Paschal victim, Paschal bread;
   With sincerity and love
   Eat we manna from above.

3 Mighty victim from the sky,
   Hell's fierce powers beneath Thee lie;
   Thou hast conquered in the fight,
   Thou hast brought us life and light:
   Now no more can death appall,
   Now no more the grave enthrall;
   Thou hast opened Paradise,
   And in Thee Thy saints shall rise.

4 Easter triumph, Easter joy,
   Sin alone can this destroy;
   From sin's power do Thou set free
   Souls new-born, O Lord, in Thee.
   Hymns of glory and of praise,
   Risen Lord, to Thee we raise;
   Holy Father, praise to Thee,
   With the Spirit, ever be.

                                R. Campbell.

Rotterdam. 7. 6.

Key of A. First Note—3.   B. Tours.

31

THE day of resurrection!
  Earth, tell it out abroad;
The Passover of gladness,
  The Passover of God.
From death to life eternal,
  From earth unto the sky,
Our Christ hath brought us over
  With hymns of victory.

2 Our hearts be pure from evil,
  That we may see aright
The Lord in rays eternal
  Of resurrection-light;
And, listening to His accents,
  May hear so calm and plain
His own "All hail," and hearing,
  May raise the victor strain.

3 Now let the heavens be joyful,
  Let earth her song begin,
The round world keep high triumph,
  And all that is therein;
Let all things seen and unseen
  Their notes together blend,
For Christ the Lord is risen,
  Our joy that hath no end.

tr. J. M. NEALE.

Easter Hymn. 7s.

Key of D. First Note—1. J. Worgan.

32

CHRIST the Lord is risen to-day,
Sons of men and angels say,
Raise your joys and triumphs high
Sing ye heavens and earth reply.

2 Love's redeeming work is done,
Fought the fight, the battle won.
Lo, our Sun's eclipse is o'er;
Lo, He sets in blood no more.

3 Vain the stone, the watch, the seal;
Christ has burst the gates of hell;
Death in vain forbids His rise:
Christ has opened paradise.

4 Lives again our glorious King:
Where, O Death, is now thy sting?
Once He died our souls to save:
Where thy victory, O grave?

5 Soar we now where Christ has led,
Following our exalted Head:
Made like Him, like Him we rise;
Ours the Cross, the grave, the skies.

CHARLES WESLEY.

Hymns

General Selections

Webb. 7. 6.

Key of B♭.   First Note—5.   G. J. Webb.

33

THE morning light is breaking;
　The darkness disappears;
The sons of earth are waking
　To penitential tears;
Each breeze that sweeps the ocean
　Brings tidings from afar,
Of nations in commotion,
　Prepared for Sion's war.

2 See heathen nations bending
　Before the God we love,
And thousand hearts ascending
　In gratitude above;
While sinners now confessing,
　The gospel call obey,
And seek the Saviour's blessing,
　A nation in a day.

3 Blest river of salvation!
　Pursue thy onward way;
Flow thou to every nation,
　Nor in thy richness stay;
Stay not till all the lowly
　Triumphant reach their home;
Stay not till all the holy
　Proclaim "The Lord is come!"
　　　　　　　　　　S. F. Smith.

Camden. L. M.

Key of E♭. First Note—1. J. B. Calkin.

34

Fling out the banner! let it float
  Skyward and seaward, high and wide;
The sun, that lights its shining folds,
  The cross, on which the Saviour died.

2 Fling out the banner! angels bend
  In anxious silence o'er the sign;
And vainly seek to comprehend
  The wonder of the love divine.

3 Fling out the banner! heathen lands
  Shall see from far the glorious sight,
And nations, crowding to be born,
  Baptize their spirits in its light.

4 Fling out the banner! sin-sick souls
  That sink and perish in the strife,
Shall touch in faith its radiant hem,
  And spring immortal into life.

5 Fling out the banner! let it float
  Skyward and seaward, high and wide,
Our glory, only in the cross;
  Our only hope, the Crucified!

6 Fling out the banner! wide and high,
  Seaward and skyward, let it shine:
Nor skill, nor might, nor merit ours;
  We conquer only in that sign.

G. W. DOANE.

Missionary Hymn. L. M.

KEY OF E♭. FIRST NOTE—1.   L. MASON.

35

FROM Greenland's icy mountains,
  From India's coral strand,
Where Afric's sunny fountains
  Roll down their golden sand;
From many an ancient river,
  From many a palmy plain,
They call us to deliver
  Their land from error's chain.

2 What though the spicy breezes
  Blow soft o'er Ceylon's isle;
Though every prospect pleases,
  And only man is vile:
In vain with lavish kindness
  The gifts of God are strown;
The heathen in his blindness
  Bows down to wood and stone.

3 Can we, whose souls are lighted
  With wisdom from on high:
Can we to men benighted
  The lamp of life deny?
Salvation, O salvation!
  The joyful sound proclaim,
Till each remotest nation
  Has learnt Messiah's Name.

4 Waft, waft, ye winds, His story,
  And you, ye waters, roll,
Till, like a sea of glory,
  It spreads from pole to pole:
Till o'er our ransomed nature,
  The Lamb for sinners slain,
Redeemer, King, Creator,
  In bliss returns to reign.

R. HEBER.

Duke Street. L. M.

KEY OF D.   FIRST NOTE—1.   J. HATTON.

36

JESUS shall reign where'er the sun
  Does his successive journeys run;
His kingdom stretch from shore to shore,
Till moons shall wax and wane no more.

2 To Him shall endless prayer be made,
  And praises throng to crown His head;
  His Name like sweet perfume shall rise
  With every morning sacrifice.

3 People and realms of every tongue
  Dwell on His love with sweetest song;
  And infant voices shall proclaim
  Their early blessings on His Name.

4 Blessings abound where'er He reigns;
  The prisoner leaps to burst his chains,
  The weary find eternal rest,
  And all the sons of want are blest.

                                I. WATTS.

Selwyn. L. M.

Key of A♭. First Note—5. Mendelssohn.

37

ARM of the Lord, awake! awake!
Put on Thy strength! the nations shake!
And let the world adoring see
Triumphs of mercy wrought by Thee.

2 Say to the heathen from Thy throne,
I am Jehovah, God alone:
Thy voice their idols shall confound,
And cast their altars to the ground.

3 Let Sion's time of favor come;
Oh, bring the tribes of Israel home;
And let our wandering eyes behold
Gentiles and Jews in Jesus' fold.

4 Almighty God, Thy grace proclaim
In every clime, of every name;
Let adverse powers before Thee fall,
And crown the Saviour Lord of all.

Wm. Shrubsole.

Cambridge. S. M.

KEY OF A. FIRST NOTE—1.   R. HARRISON.

38

WE give Thee but Thine own,
  Whate'er the gift may be:
All that we have is Thine alone,
  A trust, O Lord, from Thee.

2 May we Thy bounties thus
  As stewards true receive,
And gladly, as Thou blessest us,
  To Thee our first-fruits give.

3 Oh, hearts are bruised and dead,
  And homes are bare and cold,
And lambs for whom the Shepherd bled
  Are straying from the Fold!

4 To comfort and to bless,
  To find a balm for woe,
To tend the lone and fatherless
  Is angels' work below.

5 The captive to release,
  To God the lost to bring,
To teach the way of life and peace,
  It is a Christ-like thing.

6 And we believe Thy word,
  Though dim our faith may be;
Whate'er for Thine we do, O Lord,
  We do it unto Thee.

W. W. HOW.

Intercession. L. M.

Key of G. First Note—1.

39

O THOU through suffering perfect made,
On Whom the bitter cross was laid;
In hours of sickness, grief, and pain,
No sufferer turns to Thee in vain.

2 The halt, the maimed, the sick, the blind,
Sought not in vain Thy tendance kind;
Now in Thy poor Thyself we see,
And minister through them to Thee.

3 O loving Saviour, Thou canst cure
The pains and woes Thou didst endure;
For all who need, Physician great,
Thy healing balm we supplicate.

4 But, oh, far more, let each keen pain
And hour of woe be heavenly gain,
Each stroke of Thy chastising rod
Bring back the wanderer nearer God!

5 Oh, heal the bruisèd heart within!
Oh, save our souls all sick with sin!
Give life and health in bounteous store,
That we may praise Thee evermore!

W. W. HOW.

Melita. 8s.

Key of C.   First Note—1.   J. B. Dykes.

40

O THOU, Who madest land and sea,
  And guidest all, in all their ways,
Who hearest those who bring to Thee
  Their sacrifice of prayer and praise;
Oh, hear Thy children as they bring
Themselves a lowly offering!

2 Great God, Who with a Father's love
    Dost watch o'er all created things,
  And gatherest all, below, above,
    Beneath the shadow of Thy wings;
  Protect, we pray Thee, now, and bless
  Thy children who are fatherless.

3 Come, heavenly Father, come to-day,
    For we Thy children come to Thee,
  And Thou wilt never say us, nay,
    If come we in humility;
  New-born in Thee, O Father, bless
  Thy children who are fatherless.

4 Cast forth upon the barren strand
    Of this lone world, to Thee we fly;
  In faith and hope, we fain would stand
    Beneath Thy sheltering arm for aye;
  Stretch forth Thy hand, and pitying bless
  Thy children who are fatherless.

5 And may we all with joyful mind
    Our hearts as living offerings bring,
  The first-fruits of our life, to find
    A Father in our heavenly King;
  And learn in life and death to bless
  Thee, "Father of the fatherless."

                                G. THRING.

Broadlands. 6s.

Key of E♭.   First Note—5.   Arr. by E. F. Rimbault.

41

THOU Who with dying lips
  Thy mother didst commend
Unto the tender care
  Of Thy belovèd friend;
Thou Who by Lazarus' grave
  In human grief didst groan,
Turn, Lord, Thine eyes on those
  Left in the world alone.

2 Thou Who didst call Thy Twelve
    Their home and friends to leave,
  And in Thy kingdom all,
    Yea, more than all, receive,
  To those bereft of all,
    Thy pitying love extend,
  And let them find in Thee,
    Father, and home, and friend.

3 Thou Who didst say of old,
    "Thine orphans lend to me;
  Unto the fatherless
    I will a Father be,"
  Thy promises are sure;
    Help us to trust Thee still;
  To those who need Thee sore,
    That faithful word fulfill.

4 Thou Who in Thy still rest
    Our dear ones safe dost keep;
  Thou Who shalt bring them back
    One day from their long sleep,
  Oh, keep us by Thy grace,
    That we at last may be,
  When that bright morning dawns,
    At home with them and Thee.

E. WIGLESWORTH.

Wareham. L. M.

Key of B♭.   First Note—1.   W. Knapp.

42

FATHER of mercies, bow Thine ear,
  Attentive to our earnest prayer:
We plead for those who plead for Thee;
Successful pleaders may they be!

2 How great their work, how vast their charge!
  Do Thou their anxious souls enlarge:
  Their best acquirements are our gain;
  We share the blessings they obtain.

3 Clothe, then, with energy divine
  Their words, and let those words be Thine;
  To them Thy sacred truth reveal,
  Suppress their fear, inflame their zeal.

4 Teach them to sow the precious seed;
  Teach them Thy chosen flock to feed;
  Teach them immortal souls to gain,
  Souls that will well reward their pain.

5 Let thronging multitudes around
  Hear from their lips the joyful sound;
  In humble strains Thy grace implore,
  And feel Thy new-creating power.

6 Let sinners break their massy chains,
  Distressèd souls forget their pains;
  Let light through distant realms be spread,
  And Sion rear her drooping head.

                                B. BEDDOME.

Wareham. L. M.

Key of B♭. First Note—1. W. Knapp.

43

O LORD of hosts, Whose glory fills
   The bounds of the eternal hills,
And yet vouchsafes, in Christian lands,
To dwell in temples made with hands;

2 Grant that all we who here to-day
   Rejoicing this foundation lay,
   May be in very deed Thine own,
   Built on the precious Corner-stone.

3 Endue the creatures with Thy grace,
   That shall adorn Thy dwelling-place;
   The beauty of the oak and pine,
   The gold and silver, make them Thine.

4 To Thee they all belong; to Thee
   The treasures of the earth and sea;
   And when we bring them to Thy throne,
   We but present Thee with Thine own.

5 The minds that guide, endue with skill;
   The hands that work, preserve from ill;
   That we, who these foundations lay,
   May raise the top-stone in its day.

6 Both now and ever, Lord, protect
   The temple of Thine own elect;
   Be Thou in them, and they in Thee,
   O ever blessèd Trinity!

J. M. NEALE.

Melita. 8s.

Key of C. First Note—1.   J. B. Dykes.

44

ETERNAL Father! strong to save,
  Whose arm hath bound the restless wave
Who bidd'st the mighty ocean deep
Its own appointed limits keep;
    Oh, hear us when we cry to Thee
    For those in peril on the sea!

2 O Christ! Whose voice the waters heard
  And hushed their raging at Thy word,
Who walked'st on the foaming deep,
And calm amidst its rage didst sleep;
    Oh, hear us when we cry to Thee
    For those in peril on the sea!

3 Most Holy Spirit! Who didst brood
  Upon the chaos dark and rude,
And bid its angry tumult cease,
And give, for wild confusion, peace;
    Oh, hear us when we cry to Thee
    For those in peril on the sea!

4 O Trinity of love and power!
  Our brethren shield in danger's hour;
From rock and tempest, fire and foe,
Protect them wheresoe'er they go;
    Thus evermore shall rise to Thee
    Glad hymns of praise from land and sea.

                      W. WHITING.

Southwell. C. M.

Key of E. First Note—1.   H. S. Irons.

45

    FATHER of mercies! in Thy Word
      What endless glory shines!
    Forever be Thy Name adored
      For these celestial lines.

2 Here the Redeemer's welcome voice
    Spreads heavenly peace around;
  And life and everlasting joys
    Attend the blissful sound.

3 Oh, may these heavenly pages be
    My ever dear delight;
  And still new beauties may I see,
    And still increasing light.

4 Divine Instructor, gracious Lord,
    Be Thou forever near;
  Teach me to love Thy sacred Word,
    And view my Saviour there.

                          ANNE STEELE.

Mendon. L. M.

Key of B♭.   First Note—1.   German.

46

Lord of all being; throned afar,
  Thy glory flames from sun and star;
Centre and soul of every sphere,
Yet to each loving heart how near!

2 Sun of our life, Thy quickening ray
  Sheds on our path the glow of day;
  Star of our hope, Thy softened light
  Cheers the long watches of the night.

3 Our midnight is Thy smile withdrawn;
  Our noontide is Thy gracious dawn;
  Our rainbow arch, Thy mercy's sign;
  All, save the clouds of sin, are Thine.

4 Lord of all life, below, above,
  Whose light is truth, Whose warmth is love,
  Before Thy ever-blazing throne
  We ask no lustre of our own.

5 Grant us Thy truth to make us free,
  And kindling hearts that burn for Thee,
  Till all Thy living altars claim
  One holy light, one heavenly flame.

OLIVER W. HOLMES.

By permission and special arrangement with Houghton, Mifflin & Co.

Pass Me Not. 8. 5.

Key of E First Note—3. W. H. Doane.

47

PASS me not, O gentle Saviour,
    Hear my humble cry;
While on others Thou art smiling
    Do not pass me by.

2 Let me at a throne of mercy
    Find a sweet relief,
Kneeling there in deep contrition,
    Help my unbelief!

3 Trusting only in Thy merits,
    Would I seek Thy face,
Heal my wounded, broken spirit,
    Save me by Thy grace!

4 Thou the Spring of all my comfort,
    More than life to me,
Whom on earth have I besides Thee,
    Whom in heaven but Thee!

              MRS. F. J. CROSBY VAN ALSTYNE.

Used by permission of the Bigelow & Main Co., owners of the copyright.

Conquest. 7. 6.

Key of C. First Note—5. J. Stainer

48

O LORD, our strength in weakness,
   We pray to Thee for grace;
For power to fight the battle,
   For speed to run the race;
When Thy baptismal waters
   Were poured upon our brow,
We then were made Thy children,
   And pledged our earliest vow;

2 We then were sealed and hallowed
   By Thy life-giving word;
Were made the Spirit's temples,
   And members of the Lord;
With His own blood He bought us,
   And made the purchase sure;
His are we: may He keep us
   Sober, and chaste, and pure.

3 Conformed to His own likeness
   May we so live and die,
That in the grave our bodies
   In holy peace may lie;
And at the resurrection
   Forth from those graves may spring,
Like to the glorious body
   Of Christ, our Lord and King.

4 The pure in heart are blessed,
   For they shall see the Lord
Forever and forever
   By seraphim adored;
And they shall drink the pleasures,
   Such as no tongue can tell,
From the clear crystal river,
   And life's eternal well.

C. WORDSWORTH.

St. George or Windsor. 8.

Key of G. First Note—3.   G. J. Elvey.

49

WATCHMAN, tell us of the night,
    What its signs of promise are.
Traveller, o'er yon mountain's height,
    See that glory-beaming star.
Watchman, does its beauteous ray
    Aught of joy or hope foretell?
Traveller, yes; it brings the day,
    Promised day of Israel.

2 Watchman, tell us of the night;
    Higher yet that star ascends.
Traveller, blessedness and light,
    Peace and truth, its course portends.
Watchman, will its beams alone
    Gild the spot that gave them birth?
Traveller, ages are its own;
    See, it bursts o'er all the earth.

3 Watchman, tell us of the night,
    For the morning seems to dawn.
Traveller, darkness takes its flight;
    Doubt and terror are withdrawn.
Watchman, let thy wanderings cease;
    Hie thee to thy quiet home.
Traveller, lo! the Prince of Peace,
    Lo! the Son of God is come.

J. BOWRING.

St. Peter. C. M.

Key of E♭.   First Note—5.　　　　A. R. Reinagle.

50

Lamp of our feet, whereby we trace
　Our path when wont to stray;
Stream from the fount of heavenly grace,
　Brook by the traveller's way;

2 Bread of our souls, whereon we feed,
　True manna from on high;
Our guide and chart, wherein we read
　Of realms beyond the sky;

3 Pillar of fire, through watches dark,
　And radiant cloud by day;
When waves would 'whelm our tossing bark,
　Our anchor and our stay:

4 Word of the everlasting God,
　Will of His glorious Son;
Without Thee how could earth be trod,
　Or heaven itself be won?

5 Lord, grant us all a right to learn
　The wisdom it imparts;
And to its heavenly teaching turn,
　With simple, childlike hearts.

　　　　　　　　　　　　B. Barton.

Refuge. 7s.

Key of D.   First Note—3.   J. P. HOLBROOK

51

1 JESU, lover of my soul,
　　Let me to Thy bosom fly,
While the nearer waters roll,
　　While the tempest still is nigh,
Hide me, O my Saviour, hide,
　　Till the storm of life be past;
Safe into the haven guide,
　　Oh, receive my soul at last!

2 Other refuge have I none,
　　Hangs my helpless soul on Thee,
Leave, ah! leave me not alone,
　　Still support and comfort me:
All my trust on Thee is stayed;
　　All my help from Thee I bring;
Cover my defenseless head
　　With the shadow of thy wing.

3 Thou, O Christ, art all I want;
　　More than all in Thee I find:
Raise the fallen, cheer the faint,
　　Heal the sick, and lead the blind.
Just and holy is Thy Name;
　　I am all unrighteousness;
False and full of sin I am,
　　Thou art full of truth and grace.

4 Plenteous grace with Thee is found,
　　Grace to cover all my sin:
Let the healing streams abound,
　　Make and keep me pure within.
Thou of Life the Fountain art;
　　Freely let me take of Thee;
Spring Thou up within my heart,
　　Rise to all eternity.

　　　　　　　　CHARLES WESLEY.

Toplady. 7s.

Key of B♭. First Note—5.   T. Hastings.

52

Rock of ages, cleft for me,
   Let me hide myself in Thee;
Let the water and the blood,
From Thy side, a healing flood,
Be of sin the double cure,
Save from wrath, and make me pure.

2 Should my tears forever flow,
   Should my zeal no languor know,
All for sin could not atone,
Thou must save, and Thou alone;
In my hand no price I bring,
Simply to Thy cross I cling.

3 While I draw this fleeting breath,
   When mine eyelids close in death,
When I rise to worlds unknown,
And behold Thee on Thy throne,
Rock of ages, cleft for me,
Let me hide myself in Thee.

A. M. TOPLADY.

St. Peter. C. M.

Key of E♭.   First Note—5.   A. R. Reinagle.

53

OH, help us, Lord; each hour of need
  Thy heavenly succor give:
Help us in thought, in word, and deed,
  Each hour on earth we live!

2 Oh, help us when our spirits cry
  With contrite anguish sore;
And when our hearts are cold and dry,
  Oh, help us, Lord, the more!

3 Oh, help us through the prayer of faith
  More firmly to believe!
For still the more the servant hath,
  The more shall he receive.

4 Oh, help us, Saviour, from on high:
  We have no help but Thee.
Oh, help us so to live and die
  As thine in heaven to be!

H. H. Milman.

Penitence. 6. 5.

KEY OF D♭.   FIRST NOTE—3.   S. LANE.

54

In the hour of trial,
   Jesu, plead for me;
Lest by base denial
   I depart from Thee;
When Thou see'st me waver,
   With a look recall,
Nor for fear or favor
   Suffer me to fall.

2 With forbidden pleasures
   Would this vain world charm;
Or its sordid treasures
   Spread to work me harm;
Bring to my remembrance
   Sad Gethsemane,
Or, in darker semblance,
   Cross-crowned Calvary.

3 Should Thy mercy send me
   Sorrow, toil, and woe;
Or should pain attend me
   On my path below;
Grant that I may never
   Fail Thy hand to see;
Grant that I may ever
   Cast my care on Thee.

4 When my last hour cometh,
   Fraught with strife and pain,
When my dust returneth
   To the dust again;
On Thy truth relying,
   Through that mortal strife,
Jesu, take me, dying,
   To eternal life.

J. MONTGOMERY.

Stephanos. P. M.

Key of G. First Note—3.   H. W. Baker.

55

ART thou weary, art thou languid,
   Art thou sore distrest?
"Come to Me," saith One, "and coming,
   Be at rest."

2 Hath He marks to lead me to Him,
   If He be my guide?
"In His feet and hands are wound-prints,
   And His side."

3 Is there diadem, as monarch,
   That His brown adorns?
"Yea, a crown, in very surety,
   But of thorns."

4 If I find Him, if I follow,
   What His guerdon here?
"Many a sorrow, many a labor,
   Many a tear."

5 If I still hold closely to Him,
   What hath He at last?
"Sorrow vanquished, labor ended,
   Jordan past."

6 If I ask Him to receive me,
   Will He say me nay?
"Not till earth, and not till heaven
   Pass away."

7 Finding, following, keeping, struggling,
   Is He sure to bless?
Saints, apostles, prophets, martyrs,
   Answer, "Yes."

J. M. Neale.

Bethany. P. M.

Key of G.　First Note—3.　　　　　L. Mason.

56

NEARER, my God, to Thee,
　Nearer to Thee,
E'en though it be a cross,
　That raiseth me;
Still all my song shall be,
Nearer, my God, to Thee,
　Nearer to Thee.

2 Though like a wanderer,
　Weary and lone,
Darkness comes over me,
　My rest a stone;
Yet in my dreams I'd be
Nearer, my God, to Thee,
　Nearer to Thee.

3 There let my way appear
　Steps unto heaven;
All that Thou sendest me
　In mercy given;
Angels to beckon me
Nearer, my God, to Thee,
　Nearer to Thee.

4 Then with my waking thoughts
　Bright with Thy praise,
Out of my stony griefs
　Altars I'll raise;
So by my woes to be
Nearer, my God, to Thee,
　Nearer to Thee.

　　　　　　　　Mrs. S. F. Adams.

Olivet. 6. 6. 4. 6. 6. 6. 4.

Key of E♭. First Note—1.   L. Mason.

57

MY faith looks up to Thee,
  Thou Lamb of Calvary,
    Saviour divine!
Now hear me while I pray;
Take all my guilt away;
Oh, let me from this day
    Be wholly Thine!

2 May Thy rich grace impart
  Strength to my fainting heart,
    My zeal inspire;
As Thou hast died for me,
Oh, may my love to Thee
Pure, warm, and changeless be,
    A living fire.

3 While life's dark maze I tread,
  And griefs around me spread,
    Be Thou my guide;
Bid darkness turn to day;
Wipe sorrow's tears away;
Nor let me ever stray
    From Thee aside!

4 When ends life's transient dream,
  When death's cold, sullen stream
    Shall o'er me roll;
Blest Saviour, then in love,
Fear and distrust remove;
Oh, bear me safe above,
    A ransomed soul!

                          RAY PALMER.

Hamburg. L. M.

KEY OF F.   FIRST NOTE—1.   ARR. BY L MASON

58

MY God, permit me not to be
A stranger to myself and Thee:
Amidst a thousand thoughts I rove,
Forgetful of my highest love.

2 Why should my passions mix with earth,
And thus debase my heavenly birth?
Why should I cleave to things below,
And all my purest joys forego?

3 Call me away from flesh and sense;
Thy grace, O Lord, can draw me thence:
I would obey the voice divine,
And all inferior joys resign.

I. WATTS.

Martyrdom. C. M.

Key of A. First Note—5.   H. Wilson.

59

    LORD, when we bend before Thy throne,
        And our confessions pour,
    Teach us to feel the sins we own,
        And hate what we deplore.

2 Our broken spirits, pitying, see;
      True penitence impart;
  And let a kindling glance from Thee
      Beam hope upon the heart.

3 When we disclose our wants in prayer,
      May we our wills resign;
  And not a thought our bosom share
      Which is not wholly Thine.

4 Let faith each weak petition fill,
      And waft it to the skies,
  And teach our hearts 'tis goodness still
      That grants it, or denies.

                              J. D. CARLYLE.

St. Edith. 7. 6.

KEY OF E.   FIRST NOTE—1.   J. H. KNECHT.

60

O JESU, Thou art standing
  Outside the fast-closed door,
In lowly patience waiting
  To pass the threshold o'er:
Shame on us, Christian brothers,
  His Name and sign who bear:
Oh, shame, thrice shame upon us,
  To keep Him standing there!

2 O Jesu, Thou art knocking:
    And lo! that hand is scarred,
  And thorns Thy brow encircle,
    And tears Thy face have marred:
  O love that passeth knowledge,
    So patiently to wait!
  O sin that hath no equal,
    So fast to bar the gate!

3 O Jesu, Thou art pleading
    In accents meek and low,
  "I died for you, My children,
    And will ye treat Me so?"
  O Lord, with shame and sorrow
    We open now the door:
  Dear Saviour, enter, enter,
    And leave us nevermore.

                           W. W. HOW.

Rathburn. 8. 7.

Key of C   First Note—5.   J. Conkey.

61

IN the cross of Christ I glory,
  Towering o'er the wrecks of time;
All the light of sacred story
  Gathers round its head sublime.

2 When the woes of life o'ertake me,
    Hopes deceive, and fears annoy,
  Never shall the cross forsake me:
    Lo! it glows with peace and joy.

3 When the sun of bliss is beaming
    Light and love upon my way,
  From the cross the radiance streaming,
    Adds new lustre to the day.

4 Bane and blessing, pain and pleasure,
    By the cross are sanctified;
  Peace is there that knows no measure,
    Joys that through all time abide.

5 In the cross of Christ I glory,
    Towering o'er the wrecks of time;
  All the light of sacred story
    Gathers round its head sublime.
                              J. BOWRING.

Jesu, Magister Bone. 7. 6.

Key of F.   First Note—3.   J. B. Dykes.

62

O LAMB of God, still keep me
    Near to Thy wounded side!
'Tis only there in safety
    And peace I can abide.
What foes and snares surround me!
    What doubts and fears within!
The grace that sought and found me,
    Alone can keep me clean.

2 'Tis only in Thee hiding,
    I feel my life secure;
Only in Thee abiding,
    The conflict can endure:
Thine arm the victory gaineth
    O'er every hateful foe;
Thy love my heart sustaineth
    In all its care and woe.

3 Soon shall my eyes behold Thee,
    With rapture, face to face;
One-half hath not been told me
    Of all Thy power and grace:
Thy beauty, Lord, and glory,
    The wonders of Thy love,
Shall be the endless story
    Of all Thy saints above.

J. G. Deck.

St. Barnabas. D. S. M.

KEY OF C. FIRST NOTE—1.   ALIQUIS.

63

THOU art gone up on high
   To mansions in the skies;
And round Thy throne unceasingly
   The songs of praise arise:
   But we are lingering here,
   With sin and care opprest;
Lord, send Thy promised Comforter,
   And lead us to Thy rest.

2 Thou art gone up on high;
   But Thou didst first come down,
Through earth's most bitter agony,
   To pass unto Thy crown;
   And girt with griefs and fears
   Our onward course must be;
But only let that path of tears
   Lead us at last to Thee.

3 Thou art gone up on high;
   But Thou shalt come again,
With all the bright ones of the sky
   Attendant in Thy train.
   Lord, by Thy saving power,
   So make us live and die,
That we may stand, in that dread hour,
   At Thy right hand on high.

E. L. TOKE.

Diademata. D. S. M.

KEY OF E. FIRST NOTE—1.   G. J. ELVEY.

64

CROWN Him with many crowns,
   The Lamb upon His throne;
Hark! how the heavenly anthem drowns
   All music but its own:
   Awake, my soul, and sing
   Of Him Who died for thee,
And hail Him as thy matchless King
   Through all eternity.

2 Crown Him the Son of God
   Before the worlds began,
And ye, who tread where He hath trod,
   Crown Him the Son of Man;
   Who every grief hath known
   That wrings the human breast,
And takes and bears them for His own,
   That all in Him may rest.

3 Crown Him the Lord of Life,
   Who triumphed o'er the grave,
And rose victorious in the strife
   For those He came to save;
   His glories now we sing
   Who died, and rose on high,
Who died, eternal life to bring,
   And lives that death may die.

4 Crown Him of lords the Lord,
   Who over all doth reign,
Who once on earth, the Incarnate Word,
   For ransomed sinner slain,
   Now lives in realms of light,
   Where saints with angels sing
Their songs before Him day and night,
   Their God, Redeemer, King.

                              M. BRIDGES.

St. Cuthbert. 8. 6. 8. 4.

Key of E♭.   First Note—1.   J. B. Dykes.

65

OUR blest Redeemer, ere He breathed
 His tender, last farewell,
A Guide, a Comforter, bequeathed
 With us to dwell.

2 He came sweet influence to impart,
 A gracious, willing guest,
While He can find one humble heart
 Wherein to rest.

3 And His that gentle voice we hear,
 Soft as the breath of even,
That checks each thought, that calms each fear,
 And speaks of heaven.

4 And every virtue we possess,
 And every victory won,
And every thought of holiness
 Are His alone.

5 Spirit of purity and grace,
 Our weakness, pitying, see:
Oh, make our hearts Thy dwelling-place,
 And worthier Thee.

H. AUBER.

St. Agnes. C. M.

KEY OF G.   FIRST NOTE—3.   J. B. DYKES.

66

COME, Holy Spirit, heavenly Dove,
　　With all Thy quickening powers;
Kindle a flame of sacred love
　　In these cold hearts of ours.

2 See how we grovel here below,
　　Fond of these earthly toys:
Our souls, how heavily they go,
　　To reach eternal joys.

3 In vain we tune our lifeless songs,
　　In vain we strive to rise:
Hosannas languish on our tongues,
　　And our devotion dies.

4 Come, Holy Spirit, heavenly Dove,
　　With all Thy quickening powers;
Come, shed abroad a Saviour's love,
　　And that shall kindle ours.

　　　　　　　　　　　　　I. WATTS.

Mendon. L. M.

Key of B♭. First Note—1.   German.

67

C OME, gracious Spirit, heavenly Dove,
   With light and comfort from above;
Be Thou our guardian, Thou our guide,
O'er every thought and step preside.

2 The light of truth to us display,
  And make us know and choose Thy way;
  Plant holy fear in every heart,
  That we from Thee may ne'er depart.

3 Lead us to Christ, the living Way,
  Nor let us from His precepts stray;
  Lead us to holiness, the road
  That we must take to dwell with God.

4 Lead us to heaven, that we may share
  Fulness of joy forever there:
  Lead us to God, our final rest,
  To be with Him forever blest.

S. BROWNE.

Nicæa. P. M.

Key of E.   First Note—1.   J. B. Dykes.

68

HOLY, Holy, Holy! Lord God Almighty!
  Early in the morning our song shall rise to Thee:
Holy, Holy, Holy! merciful and mighty!
  God in Three Persons, blessèd Trinity!

2 Holy, Holy, Holy! All the saints adore Thee,
  Casting down their golden crowns around the glassy sea;
Cherubim and seraphim falling down before Thee,
  Which wert, and art, and evermore shalt be.

3 Holy, Holy, Holy! though the darkness hide Thee,
  Though the eye of sinful man Thy glory may not see,
Only Thou art holy; There is none beside Thee,
  Perfect in power, in love, and purity.

4 Holy, Holy, Holy! Lord God Almighty!
  All Thy works shall praise Thy name, in earth, and sky, and sea:
Holy, Holy, Holy! merciful and mighty!
  God in Three Persons, blessèd Trinity!

R. HEBER.

𝕬𝖊𝖘𝖑𝖊𝖞. 11. 10.

Key of B♭.   First Note—1.   Lowell Mason.

69

Hail to the brightness of Zion's glad morning :
  Joy to the lands that in darkness have lain :
Hushed be the accents of sorrow and mourning
  Zion triumphant begins its glad reign.

2 Hail to the brightness of Zion's glad morning,
    Long by the prophets of Israel foretold ;
  Hail to the millions from bondage returning ;
    Gentiles and Jews the blest vision behold.

3 Lo, in the desert rich flowers are springing ;
    Streams ever copious are gliding along ;
  Loud from the mountain-tops echoes are ringing ;
    Wastes rise in verdure, and mingle in song.

4 See, from all lands, from the isles of the ocean,
    Praise to Jehovah ascending on high ;
  Fallen are the engines of war and commotion ;
    Shouts of salvation are rending the sky.

                              THOS. HASTINGS.

By permission Thos. S. Hastings.

Moultrie. 8. 7.

Key of G.   First Note—1.   G. F. Cobb.

70

Round the Lord in glory seated
    Cherubim and seraphim
Filled His temple, and repeated
    Each to each the alternate hymn:
"Lord, Thy glory fills the heaven,
    Earth is with Thy fulness stored;
Unto Thee be glory given,
    Holy, Holy, Holy Lord."

2 Heaven is still with glory ringing,
    Earth takes up the angels' cry,
"Holy, Holy, Holy," singing,
    "Lord of Hosts, the Lord most High."
With His seraph train before Him,
    With His holy Church below,
Thus unite we to adore Him,
    Bid we thus our anthem flow:

3 "Lord, Thy glory fills the heaven,
    Earth is with Thy fulness stored;
Unto Thee be glory given,
    Holy, Holy, Holy Lord."
Thus Thy glorious Name confessing,
    With Thine angel hosts we cry
"Holy, Holy, Holy," blessing
    Thee, the Lord of Hosts most high.

R. MANT.

MOSCOW. 6.6.4.6.6.6.4.

Key of G. First Note—5. F. Giardiui.

71

Come, Thou almighty King,
  Help us Thy Name to sing,
    Help us to praise!
Father all glorious,
O'er all victorious,
Come and reign over us,
  Ancient of days!

2 Come, Thou Incarnate Word,
  Gird on Thy mighty sword;
    Our prayer attend!
Come, and Thy people bless;
Come, give Thy word success:
'Stablish Thy righteousness,
  Saviour and Friend!

3 Come, Holy Comforter,
  Thy sacred witness bear,
    In this glad hour!
Thou, Who almighty art,
Now rule in every heart,
And ne'er from us depart,
  Spirit of power!

4 To Thee, great One in Three,
  The highest praises be,
    Hence evermore;
Thy sovereign majesty
May we in glory see,
And to eternity
  Love and adore.

CHARLES WESLEY.

Paradise. P. M.

Key of E♭.   First Note—3.   J. Barnby.

72

O PARADISE, O Paradise,
  Who doth not crave for rest?
Who would not seek the happy land
  Where they that loved are blest;
    Where loyal hearts, and true,
    Stand ever in the light,
  All rapture, through and through,
    In God's most holy sight?

2 O Paradise, O Paradise,
  The world is growing old;
Who would not be at rest and free
  Where love is never cold?
    Where loyal hearts, etc.

3 O Paradise, O Paradise,
  We long to sin no more;
We long to be as pure on earth
  As on thy spotless shore;
    Where loyal hearts, etc.

4 O Paradise, O Paradise,
  We shall not wait for long;
E'en now the loving ear may catch
  Faint fragments of thy song;
    Where loyal hearts, etc.

5 Lord Jesus, King of Paradise,
  Oh, keep us in Thy love,
And guide us to Thy happy land
  Of perfect rest above;
    Where loyal hearts, etc.

F. W. FABER.

Pilgrims. P. M.

Key of E. First Note—3.   H. Smart.

73

Hark! hark, my soul! Angelic songs are swelling
O'er earth's green fields and ocean's wave-beat shore;
How sweet the truth those blessèd strains are telling
Of that new life when sin shall be no more!
    Angels of Jesus,
      Angels of light,
    Singing to welcome
      The pilgrims of the night.

2 Onward we go, for still we hear them singing,
    "Come, weary souls, for Jesus bids you come;"
And through the dark, its echoes sweetly ringing,
    The music of the Gospel leads us home.
      Angels of Jesus, etc.

3 Far, far away, like bells at evening pealing,
    The voice of Jesus sounds o'er land and sea,
And laden souls by thousands meekly stealing,
    Kind Shepherd, turn their weary steps to Thee.
      Angels of Jesus, etc.

4 Angels, sing on! your faithful watches keeping;
    Sing us sweet fragments of the songs above;
Till morning's joy shall end the night of weeping,
    And life's long shadows break in cloudless love.
      Angels of Jesus, etc.

F. W. Faber.

Materna. C. M.

Key of D♭.   First Note—5.   S. A. Ward.

74

O MOTHER dear, Jerusalem,
   When shall I come to thee?
When shall my sorrows have an end?
   Thy joys when shall I see?

2 O happy harbor of God's saints!
   O sweet and pleasant soil!
In thee no sorrow can be found,
   Nor grief, nor care, nor toil.

3 No murky cloud o'ershadows thee,
   Nor gloom, nor darksome night;
But every soul shines as the sun;
   For God Himself gives light.

4 Thy gardens and thy goodly walks
   Continually are green,
Where grow such sweet and pleasant flowers
   As nowhere else are seen.

5 Right through thy streets, with silver sound,
   The living waters flow,
And on the banks, on either side,
   The trees of life do grow.

6 Those trees for evermore bear fruit,
   And evermore do spring:
There evermore the angels are,
   And evermore do sing.

7 Jerusalem, my happy home,
   Would God I were in thee!
Would God my woes were at an end,
   Thy joys that I might see!

                                    ANON.

Urbs Beata. 7. 6.

Key of A♭.   First Note—5.   G. F. Le Jeune.

75

JERUSALEM, the golden!
  With milk and honey blest;
Beneath thy contemplation
  Sink heart and voice opprest.
I know not, oh, I know not,
  What joys await us there!
What radiancy of glory!
  What bliss beyond compare!

2 They stand, those halls of Sion,
  All jubilant with song,
And bright with many an angel,
  And all the martyr throng.
The Prince is ever in them,
  The daylight is serene;
The pastures of the blessèd
  Are decked in glorious sheen.

3 There is the throne of David;
  And there, from care released,
The shout of them that triumph,
  The song of them that feast.
And they, who with their Leader,
  Have conquered in the fight,
Forever and forever
  Are clad in robes of white.

4 O sweet and blessèd country,
  The home of God's elect!
O sweet and blessèd country,
  That eager hearts expect!
Jesu, in mercy bring us
  To that dear land of rest!
Who art, with God the Father,
  And Spirit, ever blest.

                                    J. M. Neale.

Dominus Regit Me. P. M.

KEY OF G.   FIRST NOTE—3.   J. B. DYKES.

76

THE King of love my Shepherd is,
  Whose goodness faileth never;
I nothing lack if I am His,
  And He is mine forever.

2 Where streams of living water flow
    My ransomed soul He leadeth,
  And, where the verdant pastures grow,
    With food celestial feedeth.

3 Perverse and foolish oft I strayed,
    But yet in love He sought me,
  And on His shoulder gently laid,
    And home, rejoicing, brought me.

4 In death's dark vale I fear no ill
    With Thee, dear Lord, beside me;
  Thy rod and staff my comfort still,
    Thy cross before to guide me.

5 Thou spread'st a table in my sight;
    Thy unction grace bestoweth;
  And oh, what transport of delight
    From Thy pure chalice floweth!

6 And so through all the length of days,
    Thy goodness faileth never:
  Good Shepherd, may I sing Thy praise
    Within Thy house forever.

                              HENRY W. BAKER.

Autumn. 8.

Key of A♭.   First Note—1.   Spanish Melody.

77

GUIDE me, O Thou great Jehovah,
   Pilgrim through this barren land.
I am weak, but Thou art mighty:
   Hold me with Thy powerful hand.

2 Open now the crystal fountains
   Whence the living waters flow;
Let the fiery, cloudy pillar
   Lead me all my journey through.

3 Feed me with the heavenly manna
   In this barren wilderness;
Be my sword, and shield, and banner,
   Be the Lord my Righteousness.

4 When I tread the verge of Jordan,
   Bid my anxious fears subside;
Death of death, and hell's destruction,
   Land me safe on Canaan's side.

W. WILLIAMS.

Dulce Carmen. 8. 7.

Key of A.   First Note—1.   Haydn (?).

78

    LEAD us, heavenly Father, lead us
      O'er the world's tempestuous sea;
    Guard us, guide us, keep us, feed us,
      For we have no help but Thee:
        Yet possessing
        Every blessing,
    If our God our Father be.

2 Saviour, breathe forgiveness o'er us;
    All our weakness Thou dost know;
Thou didst tread this earth before us;
    Thou didst feel its keenest woe;
      Lone and dreary,
      Faint and weary,
Through the desert Thou didst go.

3 Spirit of our God, descending,
    Fill our hearts with heavenly joy;
Love with every passion blending,
    Pleasure that can never cloy:
      Thus provided,
      Pardoned, guided,
Nothing can our peace destroy.

                                    J. EDMESTON.

Lux Benigna. 10. 4.

Key of A♭.   First Note—5.   J. B. Dykes.

79

LEAD, kindly Light, amid the encircling gloom,
    Lead Thou me on!
The night is dark, and I am far from home,
    Lead Thou me on!
Keep Thou my feet! I do not ask to see
The distant scene; one step enough for me.

2 I was not ever thus, nor prayed that Thou
    Shouldst lead me on;
I loved to choose and see my path; but now
    Lead Thou me on!
I loved the garish day; and, spite of fears,
Pride ruled my will: remember not past years.

3 So long Thy power has blest me, sure it still
    Will lead me on
O'er moor and fen, o'er crag and torrent, till
    The night is gone;
And with the morn those angel faces smile,
Which I have loved long since, and lost awhile.

J. H. Newman.

Love Divine. 8. 7.

Key of F. First Note—1.   G. F. Le Jeune.

80

L OVE divine, all love excelling,
   Joy of heaven, to earth come down!
Fix in us Thy humble dwelling,
   All Thy faithful mercies crown.

2 Jesus, Thou art all compassion,
   Pure, unbounded love Thou art;
Visit us with Thy salvation,
   Enter every trembling heart.

3 Come, almighty to deliver,
   Let us all Thy life receive;
Come to us, dear Lord, and never,
   Never more Thy temples leave.

4 Thee we would be alway blessing;
   Serve Thee as Thy hosts above;
Pray, and praise Thee without ceasing;
   Glory in Thy perfect love.

5 Finish then Thy new creation,
   Pure and spotless let us be:
Let us see our whole salvation,
   Perfectly secured in Thee:

6 Changed from glory into glory,
   Till in heaven we take our place:
Till we cast our crowns before Thee,
   Lost in wonder, love, and praise.

                           CHARLES WESLEY.

Trust. 8. 7.

Key of B♭. First Note—5.   Mendelssohn.

81

SAVIOUR, source of every blessing,
　Tune my heart to grateful lays :
Streams of mercy, never ceasing,
　Call for ceaseless songs of praise.

2 Teach me some melodious measure,
　　Sung by raptured saints above ;
　Fill my soul with sacred pleasure,
　　While I sing redeeming love.

3 Thou didst seek me when a stranger,
　　Wandering from the fold of God ;
　Thou, to save my soul from danger,
　　Didst redeem me with Thy blood.

4 By Thy hand restored, defended,
　　Safe through life thus far I've come ;
　Safe, O Lord, when life is ended,
　　Bring me to my heavenly home.

　　　　　　　　　　　　P. ROBINSON.

Watermouth. 7. 6.

Key of G.   First Note—3.   A. H. Mann

82

O SAVIOUR, precious Saviour,
  Whom yet unseen we love!
O Name of might and favor,
  All other names above!
    We worship Thee, we bless Thee,
      To Thee, O Christ, we sing;
    We praise Thee, and confess Thee
      Our holy Lord and King.

2 O bringer of salvation,
  Who wondrously has wrought,
Thyself the revelation
  Of love beyond our thought;
    We worship Thee, we bless Thee,
      To Thee, O Christ, we sing;
    We praise Thee, and confess Thee
      Our gracious Lord and King.

3 In Thee all fulness dwelleth,
  All grace and power divine;
The glory that excelleth,
  O Son of God, is Thine;
    We worship Thee, we bless Thee,
      To Thee, O Christ, we sing;
    We praise Thee, and confess Thee
      Our glorious Lord and King.

F. R. HAVERGAL.

Coronation. C. M.

Key of G. First Note—5. O. Holden.

83

All hail the power of Jesus' Name!
  Let angels prostrate fall;
Bring forth the royal diadem,
  And crown Him Lord of all!

2 Crown Him, ye martyrs of our God,
  Who from His altar call:
Extol the Stem of Jesse's rod,
  And crown Him Lord of all!

3 Hail Him, the Heir of David's line,
  Whom David, Lord did call;
The God incarnate! Man divine!
  And crown Him Lord of all!

4 Ye seed of Israel's chosen race,
  Ye ransomed of the fall,
Hail Him Who saves you by His grace,
  And crown Him Lord of all!

5 Sinners, whose love can ne'er forget
  The wormwood and the gall,
Go, spread your trophies at His feet,
  And crown Him Lord of all!

6 Let every kindred, every tribe,
  Before Him prostrate fall!
To Him all majesty ascribe,
  And crown Him Lord of all!

E. Perronet.

Brasted. 7s.

Key of G.   First Note—1.   P. Weimar.

84

CHILDREN of the heavenly King,
  As ye journey, sweetly sing!
Sing your Saviour's worthy praise,
Glorious in His works and ways!

2 We are travelling home to God,
In the way the fathers trod:
They are happy now, and we
Soon their happiness shall see.

3 Lift your eyes, ye sons of light!
Sion's city is in sight:
There our endless home shall be,
There our Lord we soon shall see.

4 Fear not, brethren; joyful stand
On the borders of your land;
Jesus Christ, your Father's Son,
Bids you undismayed go on.

5 Lord, obediently we go,
Gladly leaving all below;
Only Thou our Leader be,
And we still will follow Thee.

J. CENNICK.

Sefton. L. M.

Key of E.   First Note—3.   J. B. Calkin

85

LIFT up your heads, ye mighty gates!
Behold, the King of glory waits;
The King of kings is drawing near;
The Saviour of the world is here.

2 The Lord is just, a helper tried;
Mercy is ever at His side;
His kingly crown is holiness;
His sceptre, pity in distress.

3 Oh, blest the land, the city blest,
Where Christ the Ruler is confest!
Oh, happy hearts and happy homes
To whom this King of triumph comes!

4 Fling wide the portals of your heart!
Make it a temple, set apart
From earthly use for heaven's employ,
Adorned with prayer and love and joy.

5 Redeemer, come! I open wide
My heart to Thee: here, Lord, abide!
Let me Thy inner presence feel:
Thy grace and love in me reveal.

G. WEISSEL.

Rejoice. 6. 6. 6. 6. 8. 8.

Key of D.   First Note—5.   J. Barnby.

86

REJOICE, the Lord is King!
  Your Lord and King adore!
 Mortals, give thanks and sing,
   And triumph evermore:
Lift up your heart! lift up your voice!
Rejoice! again I say, rejoice!

2 Jesus the Saviour reigns,
   The God of truth and love:
  When He had purged our stains,
   He took His seat above.
Lift up your heart! lift up your voice!
Rejoice! again I say, rejoice!

3 He sits at God's right hand,
   Till all His foes submit,
  And bow to His command,
   And fall beneath His feet.
Lift up your heart! lift up your voice!
Rejoice! again I say, rejoice!

4 Rejoice in glorious hope!
   Jesus the Judge shall come,
  And take His servants up
   To their eternal home.
We soon shall hear the archangel's voice;
The trump of God shall sound: Rejoice!

C. WESLEY.

Dulce Carmen. 8. 7.

KEY OF A. FIRST NOTE—1.   HAYDN (?).

87

PRAISE, my soul, the King of heaven;
    To His feet thy tribute bring;
Ransomed, healed, restored, forgiven,
    Evermore His praises sing :
      Alleluia ! Alleluia !
Praise the everlasting King.

2 Praise Him for His grace and favor
    To our fathers in distress ;
Praise Him still the same as ever,
    Slow to chide, and swift to bless :
      Alleluia ! Alleluia !
Glorious in His faithfulness.

3 Father-like He tends and spares us ;
    Well our feeble frame He knows ;
In His hands He gently bears us,
    Rescues us from all our foes.
      Alleluia ! Alleluia !
Widely yet His mercy flows.

4 Angels in the height adore Him !
    Ye behold Him face to face ;
Saints triumphant bow before Him !
    Gathered in from every race.
      Alleluia ! Alleluia !
Praise with us the God of grace.

H. F. LYTE.

Hanover. 10. 11.

Key of G. First Note—5. W. Croft.

88

OH, worship the King, all glorious above!
Oh, gratefully sing His power and His love!
Our Shield and Defender, the Ancient of days,
Pavilioned in splendor, and girded with praise.

2 Oh, tell of His might. Oh, sing of His grace!
Whose robe is the light; Whose canopy, space.
His chariots of wrath the deep thunder-clouds form,
And dark is His path on the wings of the storm.

3 Thy bountiful care, what tongue can recite?
It breathes in the air, it shines in the light;
It streams from the hills; it descends to the plain,
And sweetly distils in the dew and the rain.

4 Frail children of dust, and feeble as frail,
In Thee do we trust, nor find Thee to fail;
Thy mercies, how tender! how firm to the end!
Our Maker, Defender, Redeemer, and Friend!

5 O measureless Might! ineffable Love!
While angels delight to hymn Thee above,
The humbler creation, though feeble their lays,
With true adoration shall lisp to Thy praise.

R. GRANT.

Creation. D. L. M.

KEY OF B♭. FIRST NOTE—5.　　　　　F. J. HAYDN.

89

THE spacious firmament on high,
　With all the blue ethereal sky,
And spangled heavens, a shining frame,
Their great Original proclaim.
The unwearied sun, from day to day,
Does his Creator's power display,
And publishes to every land
The work of an Almighty Hand.

2 Soon as the evening shades prevail,
　The moon takes up the wondrous tale,
　And nightly to the listening earth
　Repeats the story of her birth;
　Whilst all the stars that round her burn,
　And all the planets in their turn,
　Confirm the tidings as they roll,
　And spread the truth from pole to pole.

3 What though in solemn silence all
　Move round this dark terrestrial ball;
　What though no real voice nor sound
　Amidst their radiant orbs be found;
　In reason's ear they all rejoice,
　And utter forth a glorious voice;
　Forever singing, as they shine,
　"The Hand that made us is divine."

　　　　　　　　　JOSEPH ADDISON.

Webb. 7. 6.

Key of B♭. First Note—5.   G. J. Webb.

90

Hail to the Lord's anointed,
  Great David's greater Son;
Hail in the time appointed
  His reign on earth begun.
He comes to break oppression,
  To set the captive free:
To take away transgression,
  And rule in equity.

2 He comes with succor speedy
  To those who suffer wrong,
To help the poor and needy,
  And bid the weak be strong;
To give them songs for sighing,
  Their darkness turn to light,
Whose souls, condemned and dying,
  Were precious in His sight.

3 He shall come down like showers
  Upon the fruitful earth,
And love, joy, hope, like flowers,
  Spring in His path to birth:
Before Him on the mountains
  Shall peace, the herald, go;
And righteousness in fountains
  From hill to valley flow.

4 O'er every foe victorious,
  He on His throne shall rest;
From age to age more glorious,
  All-blessing and all-blest:
The tide of time shall never
  His covenant remove;
His name shall stand forever,
  His changeless Name of Love.

JAMES MONTGOMERY.

Vox Dilecti. C. M. D.

Key of B♭. First Note—3.   J. B. Dykes.

91

I HEARD the voice of Jesus say:
  "Come unto Me and rest;
Lay down, thou weary one, lay down,
  Thy head upon this breast."
I came to Jesus as I was,
  Weary and worn and sad;
I found in Him a resting place,
  And He has made me glad.

2 I heard the voice of Jesus say,
    "Behold, I freely give
  The living water; thirsty one,
    Stoop down, and drink, and live."
  I came to Jesus, and I drank
    Of that life-giving stream;
  My thirst was quenched, my soul revived,
    And now I live in Him.

3 I heard the voice of Jesus say,
    "I am this dark world's Light;
  Look unto Me, thy morn shall rise,
    And all thy day be bright."
  I looked to Jesus, and I found
    In Him my Star, my Sun;
  And in that Light of life I'll walk
    Till all my journey's done.

                                H. Bonar.

St. Thomas. S. M.

KEY OF G. FIRST NOTE—5. A. WILLIAMS.

92

OH, bless the Lord, my soul!
   His grace to thee proclaim!
And all that is within me join
   To bless His holy Name!

2 Oh, bless the Lord, my soul!
   His mercies bear in mind!
Forget not all His benefits!
   The Lord to thee is kind.

3 He will not always chide;
   He will with patience wait;
His wrath is ever slow to rise,
   And ready to abate.

4 He pardons all thy sins;
   Prolongs thy feeble breath;
He healeth thine infirmities,
   And ransoms thee from death.

5 He clothes thee with His love;
   Upholds thee with His truth;
And like the eagle He renews
   The vigor of thy youth.

6 Then bless His holy Name,
   Whose grace hath made thee whole,
Whose loving-kindness crowns thy days!
   Oh, bless the Lord, my soul!

JAS. MONTGOMERY.

Frederick. 11.

Key of F. First Note—5.   Geo. Kingsley.

93

I WOULD not live alway, I ask not to stay
　Where storm after storm rises dark o'er the way;
The few lurid mornings that dawn on us here
Are enough of life's woes full, enough for its cheer.

2 I would not live alway, thus fettered by sin,
Temptation without and corruption within;
E'en the rapture of pardon is mingled with fears,
And the cup of thanksgiving with penitent tears.

3 I would not live alway; no, welcome the tomb;
Since Jesus hath lain there, I dread not its gloom;
There sweet be my rest, till He bid me arise,
To hail Him in triumph descending the skies.

4 Who, who would live alway, away from his God;
Away from yon heaven, that blissful abode,
Where the rivers of pleasure flow o'er the bright plains,
And the noontide of glory eternally reigns?

5 Where the saints of all ages in harmony meet,
Their Saviour and brethren transported to greet;
While the anthems of rapture unceasingly roll,
And the smile of the Lord is the feast of the soul.

　　　　　　　　　　　　W. A. MUHLENBERG.

By permission of A. D. F. Randolph & Co.

Vienna. 7s.

Key of G.　First Note—3.　　　J. H. Knecht.

94

SONGS of praise the angels sang;
　Heaven with alleluias rang,
When Jehovah's work begun,
When He spake and it was done.

2 Songs of praise awoke the morn,
　When the Prince of Peace was born;
　Songs of praise arose, when He
　Captive lead captivity.

3 Heaven and earth must pass away;
　Songs of praise shall crown that day:
　God will make new heavens and earth;
　Songs of praise shall hail their birth.

4 And shall man alone be dumb,
　Till that glorious kingdom come?
　No; the Church delights to raise
　Psalms, and hymns, and songs of praise.

5 Saints below, with heart and voice,
　Still in songs of praise rejoice;
　Learning here, by faith and love,
　Songs of praise to sing above.

6 Borne upon their latest breath,
　Songs of praise shall conquer death;
　Then, amidst eternal joy,
　Songs of praise their powers employ.

　　　　　　　　　Jas. Montgomery.

Need. 6. 4. 6. 4. 7. 6. 7. 4.

Key of A♭.   First Note—1.   R. Lowry.

95

1 NEED Thee every hour,
  Most gracious Lord;
No tender voice like Thine
  Can peace afford.
    I need Thee, oh, I need Thee,
      Every hour I need Thee;
    Oh, bless me now, my Saviour,
      I come to thee!

2 I need Thee every hour;
    Stay Thou near by;
  Temptations lose their power
    When Thou art nigh.

3 I need Thee every hour,
    In joy or pain;
  Come quickly and abide,
    Or life is vain.

4 I need Thee every hour;
    Teach me Thy will;
  And Thy rich promises
    In me fulfill.

5 I need Thee every hour,
    Most Holy One;
  Oh, make me Thine indeed,
    Thou blessèd Son!

                    Mrs. Anna S. Hawkes.
Used by permission of the Biglow & Main Co., owners of copyright.

Retreat. L. M.

KEY OF C.   FIRST NOTE—3.   T. HASTINGS.

96

FROM every stormy wind that blows,
  From every swelling tide of woes,
There is a calm, a sure retreat;
'Tis found beneath the mercy-seat.

2 There is a place where Jesus sheds
  The oil of gladness on our heads,
  A place than all beside more sweet;
  It is the blood-stained mercy-seat.

3 There is a spot where spirits blend,
  Where friend holds fellowship with friend;
  Though sundered far, by faith they meet
  Around one common mercy-seat.

4 There, there, on eagles' wings we soar,
  And time and sense seem all no more;
  And heaven comes down, our souls to greet,
  And glory crowns the mercy-seat.

H. STOWELL.

King of Glory. 6. 6. 6. 8. 8.

Key of D♭. First Note—1. H. W. Parker.

97

1 IN loud exalted strains,
   The King of glory praise;
 O'er heaven and earth He reigns,
   Through everlasting days;
 But Sion, with His presence blest,
 Is His delight, His chosen rest.

2 O King of glory, come;
   And with Thy favor crown
 This temple as Thy home,
   This people as Thy own;
 Beneath this roof vouchsafe to show
 How God can dwell with men below.

3 Now let Thine ear attend
   Our supplicating cries;
 Now let our praise ascend,
   Accepted, to the skies:
 Now let Thy Gospel's joyful sound
 Spread its celestial influence round.

4 Here may the listening throng
   Imbibe Thy truth and love;
 Here Christians join the song
   Of seraphim above:
 Till all who humbly seek Thy face
 Rejoice in Thy abounding grace.

B. FRANCIS.

St. Thomas. S. M.

KEY OF G.   FIRST NOTE—5.   A. WILLIAMS.

98

I LOVE Thy kingdom, Lord,
  The house of Thine abode,
The Church our blest Redeemer saved
  With His own precious blood.

2 For her my tears shall fall ;
  For her my prayers ascend ;
To her my cares and toils be given,
  Till toils and cares shall end.

3 Beyond my highest joy
  I prize her heavenly ways,
Her sweet communion, solemn vows,
  Her hymns of love and praise.

4 Jesus, Thou friend divine,
  Our Saviour and our King,
Thy hand from every snare and foe
  Shall great deliverance bring.

5 Sure as Thy truth shall last,
  To Sion shall be given
The brightest glories earth can yield,
  And brighter bliss of heaven.

T. DWIGHT.

Russian Hymn. 10s.

Key of E♭.   First Note—5.   A. T. Swoff.

99

RISE, crowned with light, imperial Salem, rise!
  Exalt thy towering head and lift thine eyes!
See heaven its sparkling portals wide display,
And break upon thee in a flood of day.

2 See a long race thy spacious courts adorn :
See future sons, and daughters yet unborn,
In crowding ranks on every side arise,
Demanding life, impatient for the skies.

3 See barbarous nations at thy gates attend,
Walk in thy light, and in thy temple bend :
See thy bright altars thronged with prostrate
      kings,
While every land its joyous tribute brings.

4 The seas shall waste, the skies to smoke decay,
Rocks fall to dust, and mountains melt away ;
But fixed His word, His saving power remains ;
Thy realm shall last, thy own Messiah reigns.

                              ALEX. POPE.

Wareham. L. M.

Key of B♭.   First Note—1.   W. Knapp.

100

TRIUMPHANT Sion, lift thy head
From dust, and darkness, and the dead!
Though humbled long, awake at length,
And gird thee with thy Saviour's strength.

2 Put all thy beauteous garments on,
And let thy excellence be known:
Decked in the robes of righteousness,
The world thy glories shall confess.

3 No more shall foes unclean invade,
And fill thy hallowed walls with dread;
No more shall hell's insulting host
Their victory and thy sorrows boast.

4 God from on high has heard thy prayer,
His hand thy ruins shall repair:
Nor will thy watchful Monarch cease
To guard thee in eternal peace.

PHILIP DODDRIDGE.

St. George's, or Windsor. 7s.

Key of G.   First Note—3.   G. J. Elvey.

101

PLEASANT are Thy courts above
In the land of life and love;
Pleasant are Thy courts below
In this land of sin and woe.
Oh, my spirit longs and faints
For the converse of Thy saints,
For the brightness of Thy face,
For Thy fulness, God of grace!

2 Happy birds that sing and fly
Round Thy altars, O Most High!
Happier souls that find a rest
In a heavenly Father's breast!
Like the wandering dove, that found
No repose on earth around,
They can to their ark repair
And enjoy it ever there.

3 Happy souls! their praises flow
Ever in this vale of woe;
Waters in the desert rise,
Manna feeds them from the skies:
On they go from strength to strength
Till they reach Thy throne at length,
At Thy feet adoring fall,
Who hast led them safe through all.

4 Lord, be mine this prize to win;
Guide me through a world of sin;
Keep me by Thy saving grace;
Give me at Thy side a place.
Sun and shield alike Thou art;
Guide and guard my erring heart.
Grace and glory flow from Thee;
Shower, oh, shower them, Lord, on me!

H. T. Lyte.

Glorious Things. 8. 7.

Key of E.   First Note—3.   G. F. Le Jeune.

102

GLORIOUS things of thee are spoken,
  Sion, city of our God;
He, Whose word cannot be broken,
  Formed thee for His own abode:
On the Rock of Ages founded,
  What can shake thy sure repose?
With salvation's walls surrounded,
  Thou may'st smile at all thy foes.

2 See, the streams of living waters
    Springing from eternal love,
  Well supply thy sons and daughters,
    And all fear of want remove.
  Who can faint, when such a river
    Ever will their thirst assuage?
  Grace which, like the Lord, the giver,
    Never fails from age to age.

3 Round each habitation hovering,
    See the cloud and fire appear
  For a glory and a covering,
    Showing that the Lord is near.
  Thus deriving from their banner,
    Light by night, and shade by day,
  Safe they feed upon the manna,
    Which He gives them when they pray.

4 Blest inhabitants of Sion,
    Washed in the Redeemer's blood!
  Jesus, Whom their souls rely on,
    Makes them kings and priests to God.
  'Tis His love His people raises
    Over self to reign as kings:
  And as priests, His solemn praises
    Each for a thank-offering brings.

JOHN NEWTON.

Aurelia. 7. 6.

KEY OF E♭. FIRST NOTE—3.   S. S. WESLEY.

103

1. THE Church's one foundation
    Is Jesus Christ her Lord;
   She is His new creation
    By water and the word:
   From heaven He came and sought her
    To be His holy Bride;
   With His own blood He bought her,
    And for her life He died.

2. Elect from every nation,
    Yet one o'er all the earth,
   Her charter of salvation,
    One Lord, one Faith, one Birth;
   One holy Name she blesses,
    Partakes one holy food,
   And to one hope she presses,
    With every grace endued.

3. 'Mid toil and tribulation,
    And tumult of her war
   She waits the consummation
    Of peace for evermore;
   Till with the vision glorious
    Her longing eyes are blest,
   And the great Church victorious
    Shall be the Church at rest.

4. Yet she on earth hath union
    With God the Three in One,
   And mystic sweet communion
    With those whose rest is won:
   O happy ones and holy!
    Lord, give us grace that we
   Like them, the meek and lowly,
    On high may dwell with Thee.

S. J. STONE.

Work Song. 7. 6. 7. 5.

KEY OF F. FIRST NOTE—5. LOWELL MASON.

104

WORK, for the night is coming,
  Work through the morning hours;
Work while the dew is sparkling,
  Work 'mid springing flowers;
Work when the day grows brighter,
  Work in the glowing sun;
Work, for the night is coming,
  When man's work is done.

2 Work, for the night is coming,
  Work through the sunny noon;
Fill brightest hours with labor,
  Rest comes sure and soon:
Give every flying minute
  Something to keep in store:
Work, for the night is coming,
  When man works no more.

3 Work for the night is coming,
  Under the sunset skies;
While their bright tints are glowing,
  Work, for daylight flies:
Work, till the last beam fadeth,
  Fadeth to shine no more:
Work, while the night is darkening,
  When man's work is o'er.

ANNIE L. WALKER.

Eden. 6. 4.

KEY OF F.   FIRST NOTE—3.

105

SAVIOUR, I follow on
  Guided by Thee;
Seeing not yet the hand
That leadeth me;
Hushed be my heart and still,
Fear I no further ill;
Only to meet Thy will
My will shall be.

2 Riven the rock for me,
  Thirst to relieve;
Manna from heaven falls
Fresh every eve!
Never a want severe
Causeth my eye a tear,
But Thou dost whisper near
"Only believe."

3 Saviour I long to walk
  Closer with Thee:
Led by Thy guiding hand
Ever to be:
Constantly near Thy side,
Quickened and purified,
Living for Him who died
Freely for me.

CHARLES S. ROBINSON.

By permission of the author.

Byefield. C. M.

Key of F. First Note—1.   Thos. Hastings.

106

PRAYER is the soul's sincere desire,
  Uttered or unexpressed,
The motion of a hidden fire
  That trembles in the breast.

2 Prayer is the burden of a sigh,
  The falling of a tear,
The upward glancing of an eye,
  When none but God is near.

3 Prayer is the simplest form of speech
  That infant lips can try;
Prayer the sublimest strains that reach
  The Majesty on high.

4 Prayer is the contrite sinner's voice
  Returning from his ways,
While angels in their songs rejoice,
  And cry, "Behold he prays!"

5 Prayer is the Christian's vital breath,
  The Christian's native air,
His watchword at the gates of death;
  He enters heaven with prayer.

6 O Thou, by whom we come to God,
  The Life, the Truth, the Way,
The path of prayer Thyself hast trod;
  Lord, teach us how to pray.

JAMES MONTGOMERY.

All Saints. C. M.

Key of B♭. First Note—5. H. S. Cutler.

107

THE Son of God goes forth to war,
 A kingly crown to gain :
His blood-red banner streams afar :
 Who follows in His train?

2 Who best can drink his cup of woe,
 Triumphant over pain ;
Who patient bears his cross below,
 He follows in His train.

3 The martyr first, whose eagle eye
 Could pierce beyond the grave ;
Who saw his Master in the sky,
 And called on Him to save.

4 Like Him, with pardon on His tongue,
 In midst of mortal pain,
He prayed for them that did the wrong :
 Who follows in His train?

5 A glorious band, the chosen few,
 On whom the Spirit came :
Twelve valiant saints, their hope they knew,
 And mocked the cross and flame.

6 A noble army: men and boys,
 The matron and the maid ;
Around the Saviour's throne rejoice,
 In robes of light arrayed.

7 They climbed the steep ascent of heaven
 Through peril, toil, and pain :
O God, to us may grace be given
 To follow in their train.

R. HEBER.

Marlow. C. M.

Key of G. First Note—1. J. Chetham.

108

 Am I a soldier of the cross,
  A follower of the Lamb?
 And shall I fear to own His cause,
  Or blush to speak His name?

2 Must I be carried to the skies
  On flowery beds of ease,
 While others fought to win the prize,
  And sailed through bloody seas?

3 Are there no foes for me to face?
  Must I not stem the flood?
 Is this vile world a friend to grace,
  To help me on to God?

4 Sure I must fight if I would reign;
  Increase my courage, Lord;
 I'll bear the cross, endure the pain,
  Supported by Thy word.

5 Thy saints, in all this glorious war,
  Shall conquer, though they die;
 They view the triumph from afar,
  And seize it with their eye.

6 When that illustrious day shall rise,
  And all Thy armies shine
 In robes of victory through the skies,
  The glory shall be Thine.

I. WATTS.

Diademata. S. M.

Key of E. First Note—1. G. J. Elvey.

109

Soldiers of Christ, arise,
  And put your armor on;
Strong in the strength which God supplies,
  Through His eternal Son.

2 Strong in the Lord of Hosts,
    And in His mighty power;
  Who in the strength of Jesus trusts
    Is more than conqueror.

3 Stand then in His great might,
    With all His strength endued;
  And take, to arm you for the fight,
    The panoply of God.

4 From strength to strength go on,
    Wrestle, and fight, and pray:
  Tread all the powers of darkness down,
    And win the well-fought day.

5 That having all things done,
    And all your conflicts past,
  Ye may o'ercome, through Christ alone,
    And stand complete at last.

CHARLES WESLEY.

Lincoln. 7. 6.

Key of D. First Note—1. M. Vulpius.

110

O HAPPY band of pilgrims,
  If onward ye will tread
With Jesus as your Fellow
  To Jesus as your Head!

2 Oh, happy if ye labor
  As Jesus did for men!
Oh, happy if ye hunger
  As Jesus hungered then!

3 The cross that Jesus carried,
  He carried as your due:
The crown that Jesus weareth,
  He weareth it for you.

4 The faith by which ye see Him,
  The hope in which ye yearn,
The love that through all troubles
  To Him alone will turn;

5 The trials that beset you,
  The sorrows ye endure,
The manifold temptations
  That death alone can cure;

6 What are they but His jewels,
  Of right celestial worth?
What are they but the ladder
  Set up to heaven on earth?

7 O happy band of pilgrims,
  Look upward to the skies,
Where such a light affliction
  Shall win so great a prize!

J. M. Neale.

Beethoven. 7. 6.

KEY OF G. FIRST NOTE—3. BEETHOVEN.

III

RISE, my soul, and stretch thy wings,
  Thy better portion trace;
Rise from transitory things,
  Toward heaven, thy destined place.
Sun and moon and stars decay,
  Time shall soon this earth remove;
Rise, my soul, and haste away
  To seats prepared above.

2 Cease, my soul, oh, cease to mourn!
  Press onward to the prize;
Soon thy Saviour will return,
  To take thee to the skies:
There is everlasting peace,
  Rest, enduring rest, in heaven;
There will sorrow ever cease,
  And crowns of joy be given.

R. SEAGRAVE.

Dennis. S. M.

KEY OF F.   FIRST NOTE—3.   J. G. NAGELI.

112

OH, where shall rest be found,
   Rest for the weary soul?
'Twere vain the ocean-depths to sound,
   Or pierce to either pole.

2 The world can never give
   The bliss for which we sigh;
'Tis not the whole of life to live,
   Nor all of death to die.

3 Beyond this vale of tears
   There is a life above,
Unmeasured by the flight of years,
   And all that life is love.

4 There is a death, whose pang
   Outlasts the fleeting breath;
Oh, what eternal horrors hang
   Around the second death!

5 Lord God of truth and grace,
   Teach us that death to shun,
Lest we be banished from Thy face,
   For evermore undone.

6 Here would we end our quest:
   Alone are found in Thee
The life of perfect love, the rest
   Of immortality.

                        JAS. MONTGOMERY.

Vexillum. 6. 5.

Key of E.   First Note—3.   H. Smart.

113

BRIGHTLY gleams our banner
  Pointing to the sky,
Waving wanderers onward
  To their home on high.
Journeying o'er the desert,
  Gladly thus we pray,
And with hearts united
  Take our heavenward way.
    Brightly gleams our banner
      Pointing to the sky,
    Waving wanderers onward
      To their home on high.

2 Jesu, Lord and Master,
    At Thy sacred feet,
  Here with hearts rejoicing
    See Thy children meet:
  Often have we left Thee,
    Often gone astray;
  Keep us, mighty Saviour,
    In the narrow way.
        Brightly gleams, etc.

3 All our days direct us
    In the way we go,
  Lead us on victorious
    Over every foe:
  Bid Thine angels shield us
    When the storm-clouds lower,
  Pardon, Lord, and save us
    In the last dread hour.
        Brightly gleams, etc.

T. J. POTTER.

St. Gertrude. 6s. 5s.

KEY OF F. FIRST NOTE—5.   A. S. SULLIVAN.

114

ONWARD, Christian soldiers,
  Marching as to war,
With the cross of Jesus
  Going on before!
Christ the royal Master
  Leads against the foe;
Forward into battle,
  See, His banners go.
    Onward, Christian soldiers,
      Marching as to war,
    With the cross of Jesus
      Going on before!

2 Like a mighty army
    Moves the Church of God;
  Brothers, we are treading
    Where the saints have trod;
  We are not divided,
    All one Body we,
  One in hope and doctrine,
    One in charity.
      Onward, etc.

3 Crowns and thrones may perish,
    Kingdoms rise and wane,
  But the Church of Jesus
    Constant will remain;
  Gates of hell can never
    'Gainst that Church prevail;
  We have Christ's own promise,
    And that cannot fail.
      Onward, etc.

S. BARING GOULD.

David. 6. 5.

Key of G.   First Note—3.   T. Morley.

115

SAVIOUR, blessèd Saviour,
　　Listen while we sing;
Hearts and voices raising
　　Praises to our King.
All we have we offer,
　　All we hope to be,
Body, soul, and spirit,
　　All we yield to Thee.

2 Nearer, ever nearer,
　　Christ, we draw to Thee,
Deep in adoration
　　Bending low the knee:
Thou for our redemption
　　Cam'st on earth to die:
Thou, that we might follow,
　　Hast gone up on high.

3 Great, and ever greater
　　Are Thy mercies here,
True and everlasting
　　Are the glories there,
Where no pain, no sorrow,
　　Toil, or care, is known,
Where the angel legions
　　Circle round Thy throne.

4 Clearer still, and clearer,
　　Dawns the light from heaven,
In our sadness bringing
　　News of sins forgiven;
Life has lost its shadows;
　　Pure the light within;
Thou hast shed Thy radiance
　　On a world of sin.

　　　　　　　　　　G. THRING.

Warfare. 6. 5.

KEY OF G. FIRST NOTE—1. G. W. CHADWICK

116

FORWARD! be our watchword,
  Steps and voices joined;
Seek the things before us,
  Not a look behind:
Burns the fiery pillar
  At our army's head;
Who shall dream of shrinking,
  By our Captain led?
    Forward through the desert,
      Through the toil and fight!
    Jordan flows before us;
      Sion beams with light.

2 Glories upon glories
    Hath our God prepared,
  By the souls that love Him
    One day to be shared;
  Eye hath not beheld them,
    Ear hath never heard;
  Nor of these hath uttered
    Thought or speech a word;
      Forward! marching eastward
        Where the heaven is bright,
      Till the veil be lifted,
        Till our faith be sight.

H. ALFORD.

Ellacombe. 7. 6.

KEY OF B♭.   FIRST NOTE—5.   GERMAN.

117

COME, praise your Lord and Saviour
   In strains of holy mirth!
Give thanks to Him, O children,
   Who lived a child on earth!
He loved the little children,
   And called them to His side,
His loving arms embraced them,
   And for their sake He died.

2 O Jesus, we would praise Thee
   With songs of holy joy;
For Thou on earth didst sojourn
   A pure and spotless boy.
Make us like Thee, obedient,
   Like Thee from sin-stains free,
Like Thee in God's own temple,
   In lowly home like Thee.

3 O Jesus, we would praise Thee,
   The lowly maiden's son:
In Thee all gentlest graces
   Are gathered into one.
Oh, give that best adornment
   That Christian child can wear,
The meek and quiet spirit
   Which shone in Thee so fair!

4 O Lord, with voices lifted
   We sing our songs of praise;
Be Thou the light and pattern
   Of all our childhood's days;
And lead us ever onward,
   That while we stay below,
We may, like Thee, O Jesus,
   In grace and wisdom grow.

W. W. HOW.

Lyte. 6s. 4s.

Key of C.   First Note—3.   J. P. Holbrook.

118

JESUS, Thy name I love
All other names above,
   Jesus my Lord!
Oh, Thou art all to me!
Nothing to please I see,
Nothing apart from Thee,
   Jesus my Lord!

2 Thou blessed Son of God
Hast bought me with Thy blood,
   Jesus my Lord!
O how great is Thy love,
All other loves above,
Love that I daily prove,
   Jesus my Lord!

Jas. G. Deck.

Webb. 7. 6.

Key of B♭. First Note—5. G. J. Webb.

119

STAND up, stand up, for Jesus,
    Ye soldiers of the cross!
Lift high His royal banner!
    It must not suffer loss:
From victory unto victory
    His army shall He lead;
Till every foe is vanquished,
    And Christ is Lord indeed.

2 Stand up, stand up, for Jesus!
    The trumpet call obey!
Forth to the mighty conflict
    In this His glorious day!
Ye that are men now serve Him
    Against unnumbered foes!
Let courage rise with danger,
    And strength to strength oppose.

3 Stand up, stand up, for Jesus!
    Stand in His strength alone!
The arm of flesh will fail you,
    Ye dare not trust your own:
Put on the gospel armor,
    And watching unto prayer,
When duty calls, or danger,
    Be never wanting there!

4 Stand up, stand up, for Jesus!
    The strife will not be long:
This day, the noise of battle;
    The next, the victor's song.
To him that overcometh,
    A crown of life shall be;
He with the King of glory
    Shall reign eternally.

G. DUFFIELD.

By permission of H. H. Duffield.

Naomi. C. M.

Key of D. First Note—3. Lowell Mason.

120

Father, whate'er of earthly bliss
  Thy sovereign will denies,
Accepted at Thy throne of grace
  Let this petition rise:

2 Give me a calm and thankful heart,
    From every murmur free;
  The blessings of Thy grace impart,
    And make me live to Thee.

3 Let the sweet hope that Thou art mine
    My path of life attend:
  Thy presence through my journey shine,
    And crown my journey's end.

ANNE STEELE.

St. Crispin. 8. 8. 8. 6.

KEY OF E.   FIRST NOTE—3.   G. J. ELVEY.

121

JUST as I am, without one plea,
   But that Thy blood was shed for me,
And that Thou bidd'st me come to Thee,
   O Lamb of God, I come.

2 Just as I am, and waiting not
   To rid my soul of one dark blot,
   To Thee, Whose blood can cleanse each spot,
      O Lamb of God, I come.

3 Just as I am, though tossed about
   With many a conflict, many a doubt,
   Fightings and fears within, without,
      O Lamb of God, I come.

4 Just as I am, poor, wretched, blind;
   Sight, riches, healing of the mind,
   Yea, all I need, in Thee to find,
      O Lamb of God, I come.

5 Just as I am : Thou wilt receive,
   Wilt welcome, pardon, cleanse, relieve,
   Because Thy promise I believe,
      O Lamb of God, I come.

6 Just as I am, Thy love unknown
   Has broken every barrier down;
   Now to be Thine, yea, Thine alone,
      O Lamb of God, I come.

                                  C. ELLIOTT.

Hughton. L. M.

KEY OF D. FIRST NOTE—5.

122

HE leadeth me! oh, blessed thought!
Oh, words with heavenly comfort fraught!
Whate'er I do, where'er I be,
Still 'tis God's hand that leadeth me.

Refrain :

He leadeth me! He leadeth me!
By His own hand He leadeth me!
His faithful follower I would be,
For by His hand He leadeth me.

2 Sometimes 'mid scenes of deepest gloom,
Sometimes where Eden's bowers bloom,
By waters calm, o'er troubled sea,
Still 'tis His hand that leadeth me.

3 Lord, I would clasp Thy hand in mine,
Nor ever murmur nor repine :
Content, whatever lot I see,
Since 'tis my God that leadeth me.

4 And when my task on earth is done,
When, by Thy grace, the victory's won,
E'en death's cold wave I will not flee,
Since God through Jordan leadeth me.

J. H. GILMORE.

Used by permission of the Biglow & Main Co., owners of the copyright.

Portuguese Hymn, by M. Portugal.

11s. or Adeste Fideles.

KEY OF A. FIRST NOTE—1.   J. READING.

123

HOW firm a foundation, ye saints of the Lord,
  Is laid for your faith in His excellent word!
What more can He say than to you He hath said,
You who unto Jesus for refuge have fled?

2 Fear not, I am with thee; oh, be not dismayed!
  I, I am thy God, and will still give thee aid;
  I'll strengthen thee, help thee, and cause thee to
      stand,
  Upheld by My righteous, omnipotent hand.

3 When through the deep waters I call thee to go,
  The rivers of woe shall not thee overflow;
  For I will be with thee, thy troubles to bless,
  And sanctify to thee thy deepest distress.

4 When through fiery trials thy pathway shall lie,
  My grace, all-sufficient, shall be thy supply;
  The flame shall not hurt thee; I only design
  Thy dross to consume, and thy gold to refine.

5 The soul that to Jesus hath fled for repose,
  I will not, I will not desert to His foes;
  That soul, though all hell shall endeavor to
      shake,
  I'll never, no, never, no, never forsake.

                                        G. KEITH.

Come, Ye Disconsolate. 11. 10.

Key of D♭. First Note—5.   S. Webbe.

124

COME, ye disconsolate, where'er ye languish;
　　Come to the mercy-seat, fervently kneel;
Here bring your wounded hearts, here tell your
　　anguish;
　　Earth has no sorrow that heaven cannot heal.

2 Joy of the desolate, light of the straying,
　　Hope of the penitent, fadeless and pure,
Here speaks the Comforter, tenderly saying,
　　"Earth has no sorrow that heaven cannot
　　cure."

3 Here see the Bread of life; see waters flowing
　　Forth from the throne of God, pure from
　　above;
Come to the feast of love; come, ever knowing
　　Earth has no sorrow but heaven can remove.

　　　　　　　　　　　　　　THOS. MOORE.

Protection. 8s.

Key of F.   First Note—5   J. Pearce.

125

INSPIRER and hearer of prayer,
   Thou shepherd and guardian of Thine,
My all to Thy covenant care,
   I, sleeping or waking, resign.

2 If Thou art my shield and my sun,
   The night is no darkness to me ;
And, fast as my minutes roll on,
   They bring me but nearer to Thee.

3 A sovereign protector I have,
   Unseen, yet forever at hand ;
Unchangeably faithful to save,
   Almighty to rule and command.

4 His smiles and His comforts abound,
   His grace, as the dew, shall descend ;
And walls of salvation surround
   The soul He delights to defend.

                                  A. M. TOPLADY.

Boylston. S. M.

KEY OF C. FIRST NOTE—5. L. MASON.

126

Blest be the tie that binds
    Our hearts in Jesus' love:
The fellowship of Christian minds
    Is like to that above.

2 Before our Father's throne
    We pour united prayers;
Our fears, our hopes, our aims are one;
    Our comforts and our cares.

3 We share our mutual woes,
    Our mutual burdens bear;
And often for each other flows
    The sympathizing tear.

4 When we at death must part,
    Not like the world's, our pain;
But one in Christ, and one in heart,
    We part to meet again.

5 From sorrow, toil, and pain,
    And sin, we shall be free;
And perfect love and friendship reign
    Throughout eternity.

J. FAWCETT.

Blessed home. 6s.

Key of A♭.   First Note—3.   J. Stamer.

127

There is a blessèd home
   Beyond this land of woe,
Where trials never come,
   Nor tears of sorrow flow;
Where faith is lost in sight,
   And patient hope is crowned,
And everlasting light
   Its glory throws around.

2 There is a land of peace:
   Good angels know it well;
Glad songs that never cease
   Within its portals swell;
Around its glorious throne
   Ten thousand saints adore
Christ, with the Father One,
   And Spirit, evermore.

3 Oh, joy all joys beyond,
   To see the Lamb Who died,
And count each sacred wound
   In hands, and feet, and side!
To give to Him the praise
   Of every triumph won,
And sing through endless days
   The great things He hath done!

4 Look up, ye saints of God!
   Nor fear to tread below
The path your Saviour trod
   Of daily toil and woe!
Wait but a little while
   In uncomplaining love!
His own most gracious smile
   Shall welcome you above.

                              H. W. Baker.

Dawn.

Key of A♭.　First Note—3.　　　　E. P. Parker.

128

O NE sweetly solemn thought
　　Comes to me o'er and o'er;
I am nearer my home to-day
　　Than I ever have been before;

2 Nearer the great white throne,
　　Nearer the crystal sea,
Nearer my Father's house,
　　Where the "many mansions" be;

3 Nearer the bound of life,
　　Where we lay our burdens down;
Nearer leaving the cross,
　　Nearer gaining the crown;

4 But lying darkly between,
　　Winding down through the night,
Is the deep and unknown stream
　　To be crossed ere we reach the light.

5 Jesus, perfect my trust,
　　Strengthen the hand of my faith:
Let me feel Thee near when I stand
　　On the edge of the shore of death;

6 Feel Thee near when my feet
　　Are slipping over the brink;
For it may be I'm nearer home,
　　Nearer now than I think.

　　　　　　　　　　PHŒBE CARY.

By permission and special arrangement with Houghton, Mifflin & Co.

Spohr. C. M.

Key of G.   First Note—5.   Spohr.

129

WHILE Thee I seek, protecting Power,
   Be my vain wishes stilled;
And may this consecrated hour
   With better hopes be filled.

2 Thy love the power of thought bestowed,
   To Thee my thoughts would soar:
Thy mercy o'er my life has flowed;
   That mercy I adore.

3 In each event of life, how clear
   Thy ruling hand I see;
Each blessing to my soul more dear,
   Because conferred by Thee.

4 In every joy that crowns my days,
   In every pain I bear,
My heart shall find delight in praise,
   Or seek relief in prayer.

5 When gladness wings my favored hour,
   Thy love my thoughts shall fill;
Resigned when storms of sorrow lower,
   My soul shall meet Thy will.

6 My lifted eye, without a tear,
   The gathering storms shall see;
My steadfast heart shall know no fear;
   That heart will rest on Thee.

                         H. M. WILLIAMS.

Salamis. P. M.

Key of F.　　First Note—1.　　　　　　Greek Melody.

130

WORSHIP the Lord in the beauty of holiness,
　　Bow down before Him, His glory proclaim;
With gold of obedience and incense of lowliness,
　　Kneel and adore Him: the Lord is His name.

2 Low at His feet lay thy burden of carefulness,
　　High on His heart He will bear it for thee;
Comfort thy sorrows and answer thy prayerfulness;
　　Guiding thy steps as may best for thee be.

3 Fear not to enter His courts in the slenderness
　　Of the poor wealth thou wouldst reckon as thine;
Truth in its beauty and love in its tenderness,
　　These are the offerings to lay on His shrine.

4 These, though we bring them in trembling and fearfulness,
　　He will accept for the Name that is dear;
Mornings of joy give for evenings of tearfulness,
　　Trust for our trembling and hope for our fear.

　　　　　　　　　　　　　　J. S. B. MONSELL.

Ariel. C. P. M.

Key of E♭. First Note—5.

From Mozart
by Lowell Mason.

131

O COULD I speak the matchless worth,
O could I sound the glories forth
  Which in my Saviour shine,
I'd soar and touch the heavenly strings,
And vie with Gabriel while he sings
  In notes almost divine.

2 I'd sing the precious blood He spilt,
My ransom from the dreadful guilt
  Of sin, and wrath divine;
I'd sing His glorious righteousness,
In which all-perfect, heavenly dress
  My soul shall ever shine.

3 I'd sing the characters He bears,
And all the forms of love He wears,
  Exalted on His throne;
In loftiest songs of sweetest praise,
I would to everlasting days
  Make all His glories known.

4 Well, the delightful day will come
When my dear Lord will bring me home,
  And I shall see His face;
Then with my Saviour, Brother, Friend,
A blest eternity I'll spend,
  Triumphant in His grace.

SAMUEL MEDLEY.

Christmas. C. M.

Key of D. First Note—3. From Händel.

132

Awake, my soul, stretch every nerve,
　And press with vigor on;
A heavenly race demands thy zeal,
　And an immortal crown.

2 A cloud of witnesses around
　Hold thee in full survey;
Forget the steps already trod,
　And onward urge thy way.

3 'Tis God's all-animating voice
　That calls thee from on high;
'Tis His own hand presents the prize
　To thine uplifted eye.

4 Then wake, my soul, stretch every nerve,
　And press with vigor on;
A heavenly race demands thy zeal,
　And an immortal crown.

P. DODDRIDGE.

More Love. 6.4.6.4.6.6.4.

Key of G.   First Note—3.   T. E. Prentiss.

133

MORE love to Thee, O Christ!
  More love to Thee!
Hear Thou the prayer I make
  On bended knee;
This is my earnest plea,
More love, O Christ, to Thee,
  More love to Thee!

2 Once earthly joy I craved,
    Sought peace and rest:
  Now Thee alone I seek;
    Give what is best:
  This all my prayer shall be,
  More love, O Christ, to Thee!
    More love to Thee!

3 Let sorrow do its work,
    Send grief and pain;
  Sweet are Thy messengers,
    Sweet their refrain,
  When they can sing with me,
  My love, O Christ, to Thee,
    More love to Thee.

4 Then shall my latest breath
    Whisper Thy praise;
  This be the parting cry
    My heart shall raise,
  This still its prayer shall be,
  More love, O Christ, to Thee,
    More love to Thee!

                    Mrs. E. Prentiss.

Printed by permission.

Greenville. 8. 7. 4.

KEY OF F.   FIRST NOTE—1.   J. J. ROUSSEAU.

134

LORD, dismiss us with Thy blessing,
   Fill our hearts with joy and peace;
Let us each, Thy love possessing,
   Triumph in redeeming grace:
     O refresh us,
Travelling through this wilderness.

2 Thanks we give, and adoration,
   For Thy gospel's joyful sound:
May the fruits of Thy salvation
   In our hearts and lives abound;
     May Thy presence
With us evermore be found.

3 So, whene'er the signal's given,
   Us from earth to call away,
Borne on angel's wings to heaven,
   Glad the summons to obey,
     May we ever
Reign with Christ in endless day.

                  JOHN FAWCETT.

Old Hundred. L. M.

KEY OF G.   FIRST NOTE—6.   G. FRANC.

PRAISE God, from whom all blessings flow;
   Praise Him, all creatures here below;
Praise Him above, ye heavenly host;
Praise Father, Son, and Holy Ghost.

                  THOMAS KEN.

Chants

Venite, exultemus Domino.

1 O come, let us síng | unto . the | Lord : let us heartily rejóice in the | strength of | our sal | vation.

2 Let us come before his présence with | thanks . = | giving : and shów ourselves | glad in | him with | psalms.

3 For the Lórd is a | great . = | God : and a gréat | King a | bove all | gods.

4 In his hand are all the córners | of the | earth : and the stréngth of the | hills is | his . = | also.

5 The sea is hís | and he | made it : and his hánds pre | pared . the | dry . = | land.

6 O come let us wórship and | fall . = | down : and knéel be | fore the | Lord our | Maker.

7 For hé is the | Lord our | God : and we are the people of his pasture * ánd the | sheep of | his . = | hand.

8 O worship the Lórd in the | beauty . of | holiness : let the whole eárth | stand in | awe of | him.

9 For he cometh, for he cómeth to | judge the | earth : and with righteousness to judge the wórld and the | people | with his | truth.

Glory be to the Fáther | and . to the | Son : ánd | to the | Holy | Ghost ;

As it was in the beginning * is nów, and | ever | shall be : wórld without | end . = | A . = | men.

Te Deum.

135

   F. f We práise | thee O | God : we acknówl- edge | thee to | be the | Lord.
   F. 2 All the éarth doth | worship | thee : thé | Father | ever- | -lasting.
   3 To thee all A'ngels | cry a- | -loud : the Héavens, and | all the | Powers there- | -in.
   4 To thee Chérubin and | Seraph- | -in : cón-| tinual- | -ly do | cry,
   5 Hóly | Holy | Holy : Lórd | God of | Saba- |-oth;
   6 Heaven and earth are fúll of the | Majes- | -ty : óf | thy | Glo- | -ry.
   7 The glorious cómpany | of . the A- | -pos- tles : práise | — | — | thee.
   8 The goodly féllowship | of the | Prophets : práise | — | — | thee.
   2nd part. 9 The nóble | army . of | Martyrs : práise | — | — | thee.
   10 The holy Chúrch throughout | all the | world : dóth ac- | -know- | -ledge | thee;
   11 Thé | Fa- | -ther : óf an | infinite | Majes- | -ty;
   12 Thíne ad- | -orable | true : ánd | on- | — -ly | Son;
   13 A'lso the | Holy | Ghost : thé | Com- | -fort- | -er.
   14 Thóu art the | King of | Glory : O' | — | — | Christ.
   15 Thou art the éver- | -lasting | Son : óf | — the | Fa- | -ther.

mf 16 When thou tookest upón thee to de- | -liver | man : thou didst humble thysélf to be | born | of a | Virgin.

17 When thou hadst overcóme the | sharpness . of | death : thou didst open the Kíngdom of | Heaven to | all be- | -lievers.

18 Thou sittest at the ríght | hand of | God : ín the | Glory | of the | Father.

19 We belíeve that | thou shalt | come : tó | be | our | Judge.

20 We therefore práy thee | help thy | servants : whom thou hast redéemed | with thy | precious | blood.

21 Make them to be númbered | with thy | Saints : ín | glory | ever- | -lasting.

22 O Lórd | save thy | people : ánd | bless thine | herit- | -age.

23 Góv- | — -ern | them : ánd | lift them | up for | ever.

F. f 24 Dáy | by | day : wé | magni- | -fy | thee ;

F. 25 A'nd we | worship . thy | Name : éver | world with- | -out | end.

mf 26 Vóuch- | -safe O | Lord : to kéep us this | day with- | -out | sin.

27 O Lórd have | mercy . up- | -on us : háve | mer- | -cy up- | -on us.

28 O Lord let thy mércy | be up- | -on us : ás our | trust | is in | thee.

29 O Lord in thée | have I | trusted : lét me | never | be con- | -founded.

These Chants are from the Cathedral Psalter by permission of Messrs. Novello, Ewer & Co.

Gloria in Excelsis.

136

1 Glory be to | God on | high, | and on earth | peace, good- | will- - towards | men.

2 We praise thee, we bless thee, we | worship | thee, ‖ we glorify thee, we give thanks to | thee for | thy great | glory.

3 O Lord God, | heavenly | King, | God the | Father | Al- — | mighty.

4 O Lord, the only begotten Son, | Jesus | Christ; O Lord God, Lamb of God, Son | of the | Father,

5 That takest away the | sins- -of the | world, ‖ have mercy | upon | us.

6 Thou that takest away the | sins- -of the | world, ‖ have mercy | upon | us.

7 Thou that takest away the | sins- -of the | world, re- | ceive our | prayer.

8 Thou that sittest at the right hand of | God the | Father, | have mercy | upon | us.

9 For thou | only- -art | holy : ‖ thou | only | art the | Lord :

10 Thou only, O Christ, with the | Holy | Ghost, ‖ art most high in the | glory- -of | God the | Father, ‖ A- | men.

Benedictus.

137

F.mf Blessed be the Lórd | God of | Israel : for he hath vísited | and re- | deemed . his | people ;

F. 2 And hath raised up a míghty sal- | -vation | for us : in the hóuse | of his | servant | David ;

3 As he spake by the móuth of his | holy | Prophets : which have béen | since the | world be- | -gan ;

4 That we should be sáved | from our | enemies : and fróm the | hand of | all that | hate us ;

5 To perform the mercy prómised | to our | forefathers : ánd to re- | -member . his | holy | Convenant ;

6 To perform the oath which he swáre to our | forefather | Abraham : thát | he would | give | us ;

7 That we being delivered out of the hánd | of our | enemies : might sérve | him with- | -out | fear ;

8 In holiness and ríghteous- | -ness be- | -fore him : áll the | days | of our | life.

9 And thou Child shalt be called the Próphet | of the | Híghest : for thou shalt go before the face of the Lórd | to pre- | pare his | ways ;

10 To give knowledge of salvátion | unto . his | people : fór the re- | -mission | of their | sins,

11 Through the tender mércy | of our | God : whereby the day-spring fróm on | high hath | visited | us ;

12 To give light to them that sit in darkness* and ín the | shadow . of | death : and to guide our féet | into . the | way of | peace.

F. f Glory be to the Fáther, | and . to the | Son : ánd | to the | Holy | Ghost ;

F. As it was in the beginning* is nów, and | ever | shall be : world without | end. | A- | -men.

Jubilate Deo.

138   Psalm C.

f O be joyful in the Lórd | all ye | lands : serve the Lord with gladness* and come befóre his | presence | with a | song.

  2 Be ye sure that the Lórd | he is | God : it is he that hath made us and not we ourselves* we are his people, ánd the | sheep of | his | pasture.

  3 O go your way into his gates with thanksgiving * and ínto his | courts with | praise : be thankful unto hím, and | speak good | of his | Name.

mf 4 For the Lord is gracious * his mércy is | ever- | -lasting : and his truth endureth from géner- | -ation . to | gener- | -ation.

An asterisk (*) is a direction to take breath.

Magnificat.

139

F. mf My soul doth mágni- | -fy the | Lord : and my spirit háth re- | -joiced . in | God my | Saviour.
F. 2 Fór he | hath re- | -garded : the lówliness | of his | hand- | -maiden.
   3 Fór be- | -hold from | henceforth : áll gener- | -ations . shall | call me | blessed.
   4 For he that is mighty hath | magnified | me : ánd | holy | is his | Name.
_{2nd part.} 5 And his mércy is on | them that | fear him : throughóut | all | gener- | -ations.
   6 He hath showed stréngth | with his | arm : he hath scattered the proud in the imágin- | -ation | of their | hearts.
   7 He hath put down the míghty | from their | seat : and háth ex- | -alted . the | humble . and | meek.
   8 He hath filled the húngry with | good | things : and the rích he hath | sent | empty . a- | -way.
   9 He remembering his mercy hath hólpen his | servant | Israel : as he promised to our forefathers ∗ A'braham | and his | seed for | ever.
F. f Glory be to the Fáther, | and . to the | Son : ánd | to the | Holy | Ghost ;
F. As it was in the beginning ∗ is nów, and | ever | shall be : wórld without | end. | A- | -men

Cantate Domino.

140   Psalm XCVIII.

F. f O sing unto the Lórd a | new | song : for hé hath | done | marvellous | things.

F. 2 With his own right hand ✶ and with his | holy | arm : háth he | gotten . him- | -self the | victory.

3 The Lord declàred | his sal- | -vation : his righteousness hath he openly shówed in the | sight | of the | heathen.

4 He hath remembered his mercy and truth, tóward the | house of | Israel : and all the ends of the world have séen the sal- | -vation | of our | God.

5 Show yourselves joyful unto the Lórd | all ye | lands : sing, re- | -joice and | give | thanks.

6 Praise the Lórd up- | -on the | harp : sing to the hárp with a | psalm of | thanks- | -giving.

7 With trúmpets | also and | shawms : O show yourselves jóyful be- | -fore the | Lord the | King.

8 Let the sea make a noise ✶ and áll that | therein | is : the round wórld, and | they that | dwell there- | -in.

9 Let the floods clap their hands ✶ and let the hills be joyful togéther be- | -fore the | Lord : for he | cometh . to | judge the | earth.

10 With righteousness shall he | judge the | world : ánd the | people | with | equity.

F. f Glory be to the Fáther, | and . to the | Son : ánd | to the | Holy | Ghost ;

F. As it was in the beginning ✶ is nów, and | ever | shall be : wórld without | end. | A- | -men.

Bonum Est Confiteri.

141   Psalm XCII.

f It is a good thing to give thánks | unto . the | Lord : and to sing praises únto thy | Name | O most | Highest ;

2 To tell of thy loving-kindness éarly | in the | morning : and of thy trúth | in the | night- | -season ;

3 Upon an instrument of ten strings * ánd up- | -on the | lute : upon a loud instrument | ánd up- | -on the | harp.

4 For thou, Lord, hast made me glád | through thy | works : and I will rejoice in giving praise, for the óper- | ations | of thy | hands.

Deus Misereatur.

142   Psalm LXVII.

F.mf God be merciful únto | us and | bless us : and show us the light of his countenance ✶ ánd be | merciful | unto | us ;

F. 2 That thy way may be knówn up- | -on ‖ earth : thy sáving | health a- | -mong all | nations.

F. 3 Let the people práise | thee O | God : yéa let | all the | people | praise thee.

4 O let the nations rejóice | and be | glad : for thou shalt judge the folk righteously ✶ and góvern the | nations . up- | -on | earth.

F. 5 Let the people práise thee | O | God : yéa let | all the | people | praise thee.

6 Then shall the éarth bring | forth her | increase : and God, even our own Gód, shall | give | us his | blessing.

_{2nd part.} 7 Gód | shall | bless us : and all the ends of the | world shall | féar | him.

F. f Glory be to the Fáther, | and . to the | Son : ánd | to the | Holy | Ghost ;

F. As it was in the beginning ✶ is nów, and | ever | shall be : wórld without | end. | A- | -men.

Benedic Anima Mea.

143   Psalm CIII.

F. f Praise the Lórd | O my | soul : and all that is withín me | praise his | holy | Name.

F. 2 Praise the Lórd | O my | soul : ánd for- | -get not | all his | benefits ;

3 Who forgíveth | all thy | sin : and héaleth | all | thine in- | -firmities ;

4 Who saveth thy life | from de- | -struction : and crowneth thée with | mercy . and | loving-| -kindness ;

5 O praise the Lord, ye angels of his * yé that ex- | -cel in | strength : ye that fulfil his commandment * and hearken ínto the | voice | of his | word.

6 O praise the Lórd, all | ye his | hosts : ye sérvants of | his that | do his | pleasure.

2nd part. 7 O speak good of the Lórd, all ye works of his * in all pláces of | his do- | -minion : práise thou the | Lord | O my | soul.

F. f Glory be to the Fáther, | and . to the | Son : ánd | to the | Holy | Ghost ;

F. As it was in the beginning * is nów, and | ever| shall be : wórld without | end. | A- | -men.

Psalm of Thanksgiving.

144

F. f O Praise the Lord * for it is a good thing to sing práises | unto . our | God : yea a joyful and pleasant thing it | is to | be | thankful.

F. 2 The Lord doth búild | up Je- | -rusalem : and gather togéther the | out- | -casts of | Israel.

3 He healeth thóse that are | broken . in | heart: and gíveth | medicine . to | heal their | sickness.

4 He telleth the númber | of the | stars : and cálleth them | all | by their | names.

5 Great is our Lord * and gréat | is his | power : yéa, and his | wisdom | is | infinite.

6 The Lórd setteth | up the | meek : and bringeth the ungódly | down | to the | ground.

7 O sing unto the Lórd with | thanks- | -giving : sing praises upón the | harp | unto . our | God.

8 Who covereth the heaven with clouds * and prepareth ráin | for the | earth : and maketh the grass to grow upon the mountains * and hérb | for the | use of | men.

9 Who giveth fódder | unto . the | cattle : and feedeth the yóung | ravens . that | call up- | -on him.

10 He hath no pleasure in the stréngth | of an | horse : neither delígheth | he in | any . man's | legs.

11 But the Lord's delíght is in | them that | fear him : and pút their | trust | in his | mercy.

12 Praise the Lórd | O Je- | -rusalem : práise thy | God | O | Sion.

13 For he hath made fast the bárs | of thy | gates : ánd hath | blessed . thy | children . with- | -in thee.

14 He makéth péace | in thy | borders : and filleth thee | with the | flour of | wheat.

Domini Est Terra.

Psalm XXIV.

145

f The earth is the Lord's * and áll that | therein | is : the compass of the wórld, and | they that | dwell there- | -in.

2 For he hath fóunded it up- | -on the | seas : and prepáred | it up- | -on the | floods.

3 Who shall ascend into the hill | of the | Lord : or who shall rise úp | in his | holy | place?

4 Even he that hath clean hánds and a | pure | heart : and that hath not lift up his mind unto vanity * nor swórn | to de- | -ceive his | neighbour.

5 He shall receive the bléssing | from the | Lord : and righteousness fróm the | God of | his sal- | -vation.

6 This is the generátion of | them that | seek him : even of thém that | seek thy | face O | Jacob.

7 Lift up your heads O ye gates * and be ye lift up ye éver- | -lasting | doors : and the Kíng | of | glory | shall come | in.

8 Whó is the | King of | glory : it is the Lord strong and mighty * éven the | Lord | mighty . in | battle.

9 Lift up your heads O ye gates * and be ye lift up ye éver- | -lasting | doors : and the Kíng of | glory | shall come | in.

10 Whó is the | King of | glory : even the Lord of hósts | he . is the | King of | glory.

Dominus Regit Me.

Psalm XXIII.

146

1 The Lórd | is my | shepherd ‖ I | shall— | — not | want.

2 He maketh me to lie dówn in | green— | pastures : ‖ he léadeth me be- | -side the | still —| waters.

3 Hé re- | -storeth my | soul : ‖ he leadeth me in the paths of ríghteousness | for his | name's— | sake.

4 Yea, though I walk through the valley of the shadow of déath, I will | fear no evil ; ‖ for thou art with me ; thy ród and thy | staff, they | comfort | me.

5 Thou preparest a table before me in the présence | of mine | enemies ; ‖ thou anointest my head with óil ; my | cup — | runneth | over.

6 Surely goodness and mercy shall follow me áll the | days — of my | life, ‖ and I will dwell in the hóuse of the | Lord for- | -ev— | -er.

Psalm CXXI

147

1 I will lift up mine éyes | unto—the | hills, ‖ fróm | whence— | cometh—my | help.

2 My help cómeth | from the | Lord ‖ whích | made— | heaven—and | earth.

3 He will not suffer thy fóot | to be | movéd ‖ hé that | keepeth—thee | will not | slumber.

4 Behold, hé that | keepeth | Israel ‖ shall | neither | slumber nor | sleep.

5 The Lórd | is thy | keeper ; ‖ the Lord is thy sháde up- | -on thy | right— | hand.

6 The sun shall not smíte | thee by | day, ‖ nór the | moon— | by— | night.

7 The Lord shall presérve thee | from all | evil ; ‖ hé | shall pre- | -serve thy | soul.

8 The Lord shall preserve thy going óut and thy | com-ing | in ; ‖ from this time fórth, and | even—for- | -ev-er- | -more.

Psalm XIX.

148

The heavens decláre the | glory . of | God:
and the fírmament | sheweth . his | handy- | -work.

2 One dáy | telleth . an- | -other : and one nght | certi- | -fieth . an- | -other.

3. There is neíther | speech nor | language :
bút their | voices . are | heard a- | -mong them.

4 Their sound is gone óut into | all | lands :
and their wórds into the | ends | of the | world.

5 In them hath he set a tábernacle | for the | sun : which cometh forth as a bridegroom out of his chamber * and rejóiceth as a | giant . to | run his | course.

6 It goeth forth from the uttermost part of the heaven * and runneth about unto the énd of | it a- | -gain : and there is nothing híd | from the | heat there- | -of.

7 The law of the Lord is an undefiled láw,
con- | -verting . the | soul : the testimony of the Lord is sure * and gíveth | wisdom | unto . the | simple.

8 The statutes of the Lord are ríght and re- | -joice the | heart : the commandment of the Lord is pure * and gíveth | light | unto . the | eyes.

9 The fear of the Lord is cléan and en- | -dureth . for | ever : the judgments of the Lord are trúe, and | righteous | alto- | -gether.

10 More to be desired are they than gold * yéa than | much fine | gold : sweeter álso than | honey | and the | honeycomb.

11 Moreover, by thém is thy | servant | taught :
and in kéeping of them | there is | great re- | -ward.

mp 12 Who can téll how | oft . he of- | -fendeth :
O cleanse thou mé | from my | secret | faults.

13 Keep thy servant also from presumptuous sins * lest they get the domínion | over | me : so

163

shall I be undefiled, and innocent | from the | great of- | -fence.

14 Let the words of my mouth ∗ and the meditátion | of my | heart : be álway ac- | ceptable | in thy | sight,

15 O′|— | Lord : my | strength and ! my re- | -deemer.

The Lord's Prayer.

CHANT.

149

OUR Father, who art in heaven,
   Hallowed be thy name,
     Thy kingdom come,
Thy will be done on earth
   As it is in heaven.
Give us this day our daily bread,
   And forgive us our trespasses,
As we forgive those who trespass against us;
And lead us not into temptation,
   But deliver us from evil,
   For thine is the kingdom,
And the power, and the glory,
   Forever and ever. Amen.

Patriotic Selections

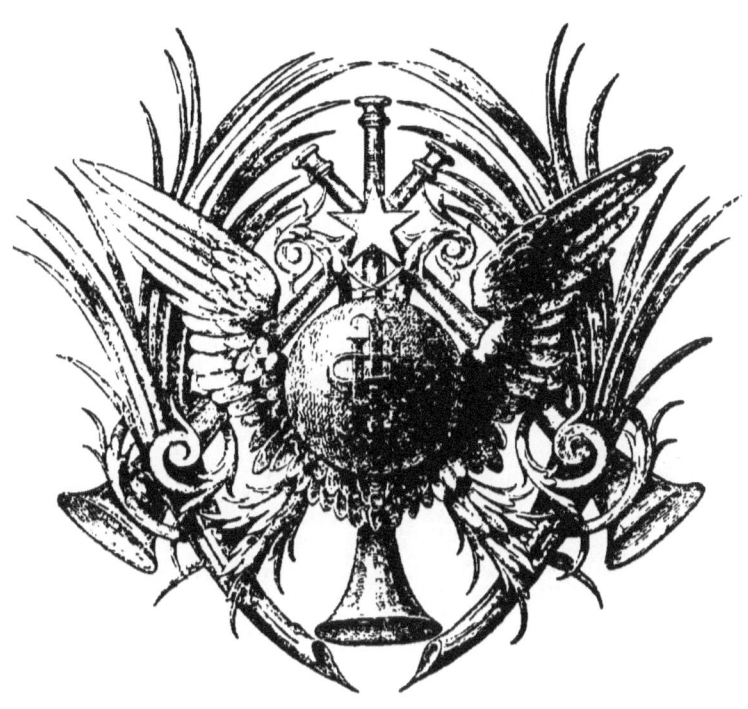

Blest of God.

Key of G. First Note—1. J. TROWBRIDGE.

150

BLEST of God, the God of Nations,
  Hail! Columbia! Hail to thee!
Let the lips of happy millions
  Sound the notes of Jubilee!
Northern breezes waft the anthem!
  South winds blowing, swell the strain!
While the Rockies catch the echo,
  Sending back the glad refrain.

2 Faith, a pilgrim, rocked thy cradle,
    By the sullen, wintry sea,
  And the patriot arm of valor
    From each foe defended thee.
  Dews of youth still brightly sparkle
    On thy brow so queenly fair,
  Yet what name, in song or story,
    Can to-day with thine compare?

3 Starry banners, proudly waving,
    Greet the rosy morning light,
  From Katahdin's cloud-capp'd summit,
    To Tacoma's snow-crown'd height,
  Fertile plains and teeming waters
    Fill thy lap with wealth untold,
  But thy children's fond devotion
    Far outweighs thy treasured gold.

4 Filial souls, with love adore thee,
    Where the palmettos arch the glade,
  Loyal sons proclaim thy glory,
    'Neath the mountain pine-tree shade:
  One in heart, with voices blending,
    North and South, your tribute raise!
  Sound aloud the mighty chorus!
    Shout! O shout! Columbia's praise!

GRANVILLE PUTNAM.

Published by permission of the author.
Musical settings are published by Messrs. Oliver Ditson & Co.

America.

Key of G.   First Note—1.   Henry Carey.

151

My country! 'tis of thee,
　　Sweet land of liberty,
　Of thee I sing;
Land where my fathers died!
Land of the pilgrims' pride!
From every mountain side
　　Let freedom ring!

2 My native country, thee—
　Land of the noble free—
　　Thy name I love!
I love thy rocks and rills,
Thy woods and templed hills;
My heart with rapture thrills
　　Like that above.

3 Let music swell the breeze,
　And ring from all the trees,
　　Sweet freedom's song;
Let mortal tongues awake;
Let all that breathe partake;
Let rocks their silence break,
　　The sound prolong.

4 Our fathers' God! to Thee,
　Author of liberty,
　　To Thee we sing;
Long may our land be bright
With freedom's holy light;
Protect us by Thy might,
　　Great God, our King!

　　　　　　　　　　SAMUEL F. SMITH.

The Star Spangled Banner.

Key of A. First Note—5.   Francis Scott Key.

152

OH, say, can you see, by the dawn's early light,
  What so proudly we hail'd at the twilight's last gleaming,
Whose broad stripes and bright stars, thro' the perilous fight,
  O'er the ramparts we watch'd were so gallantly streaming?
And the rocket's red glare, the bombs bursting in air,
Gave proof thro' the night that our flag was still there.

CHORUS.

Oh, say does that star-spangled banner yet wave
O'er the land of the free, and the home of the brave.

On the shore dimly seen thro' the mists of the deep,
  Where the foe's haughty host in dread silence reposes,
What is that which the breeze, o'er the towering steep,
  As it fitfully blows, half conceals, half discloses?
Now it catches the gleam of the morning's first beam,
In full glory reflected, now shines on the stream:

CHORUS.

'Tis the star-spangled banner: Oh, long may it wave
O'er the land of the free, and the home of the brave.

And where is that band who so vauntingly swore,
  That the havoc of war and the battle's confusion,
A home and a country should leave us no more?
  Their blood has wash'd out their foul footstep's pollution.
No refuge could save the hireling and slave,
From the terror of flight or the gloom of the grave:

CHORUS.

And the star-spangled banner in triumph doth wave
O'er the land of the free, and the home of the brave.

Oh, thus be it ever when freemen shall stand,
  Between their loved home and wild war's desolation;
Blest with victory and peace, may the heav'n rescued land
  Praise the pow'r that hath made and preserved us a nation!
Then conquer we must, when our cause it is just,
And this be our motto: "In God is our trust!"

CHORUS.

And the star-spangled banner in triumph shall wave
O'er the land of the free, and the home of the brave.

Hail, Columbia.

Key of G.   First Note—1.   —Phyla.

153

Hail, Columbia! happy land!
   Hail, ye heroes, heav'n-born band!
Who fought and bled in Freedom's cause,
Who fought and bled in Freedom's cause,
And when the storm of war was gone,
Enjoyed the peace your valor won.
Let independence be our boast,
Ever mindful what it cost;
Ever grateful for the prize,
Let its altars reach the skies.

CHORUS.

Firm, united, let us be,
Rallying round our liberty!
As a band of brothers joined,
Peace and safety we shall find.

Immortal patriots, rise once more!
Defend your rights, defend your shore;
Let no rude foe, with impious hand,
Let no rude foe, with impious hand,
Invade the shrine where sacred lies,
Of toil and blood the well-earned prize;
While off'ring peace sincere and just,
In Heav'n we place a manly trust,
That truth and justice shall prevail,
And ev'ry scheme of bondage fail.

CHORUS.

Firm, united, let us be, etc.

JOSEPH HOPKINSON.

The Red, White and Blue.

Key of A♭.   First Note—5.   D. F. Shaw.

154

OH, Columbia, the gem of the ocean,
  The home of the brave and the free,
The shrine of each patriot's devotion,
  A world offers homage to thee;
Thy mandates make heroes assemble,
  When Liberty's Form stands in view;
Thy banners make tyranny tremble,
  When borne by the red, white and blue,

Chorus.

  When borne by the red, white and blue,
  When borne by the red, white and blue,
  Thy banners make tyranny tremble,
  When borne by the red, white and blue.

When war wing'd its wide desolation,
  And threaten'd the land to deform,
The ark then of freedom's foundation,
  Columbia, rode safe thro' the storm:
With the garlands of vict'ry around her,
  When so proudly she bore her brave crew,
With her flag proudly floating before her,
  The boast of the red, white and blue,

The star spangled banner bring hither,
  O'er Columbia's true sons let it wave;
May the wreaths they have won never wither,
  Nor its stars cease to shine on the brave;
May the service united ne'er sever,
  But hold to their colors so true;
The army and navy forever,
  Three cheers for the red, white and blue.

The Breaking Waves Dashed High.

KEY OF D. FIRST NOTE—5.   ARR. MISS BROWNE.

155

    THE breaking waves dash'd high,
      On a stern and rock-bound coast,
    The woods against a stormy sky,
      Their giant branches tossed ;
    The heavy night hung dark,
      The hills and waters o'er,
    When a band of exiles moor'd their bark
      On wild New England's shore.

2 Not as the conqueror comes,
    They, the true-hearted came ;
  Not with the roll of the stirring drums,
    Or trump that sings of fame,
  Nor as the flying come,
    In silence and in fear,
  They shook the depths of deserts gloom
    With hymns of lofty cheer.

3 Amid the storm they sang,
    The stars heard and the sea !
  The sounding aisles of woodland rang
    With anthems of the free.
  The ocean eagle soared
    O'er rolling wave's white foam,
  The rocking pines in forest roar'd,
    To bid them welcome home.

4 What sought they thus afar ?
    Bright jewels of the mine ?
  The wealth of seas, the spoils of war ?
    They sought a faith's pure shrine !
  Ay, call it holy ground,
    The soil where first they trod :
  They left unstained what there they found,
    Freedom to worship God.

                                    FELICIA HEMANS.

March of the Men of Columbia.

Key of A♭.   First Note—1.   Joseph Barnby.

156

FROM the hillside, from the hollow,
  Do you hear like rushing billow,
Wave on wave, that surging follow,
  Till they shake the ground?
Hail this day of happy omen,
'Tis the tramp of gath'ring freemen,
Labor's hosts of sturdy yeomen,
  Swell th' exulting sound.
Loose the folds asunder,
Flag we rally under;
  The placid sky, now bright on high,
  We'll rend with shouts like thunder.

CHORUS.

Onward press, our country needs us;
Onward press, 'tis glory leads us;
Hark! the watchword high that speeds us,
  Freedom, God, and Right.

Lo! the tyrant's days are numbered,
Liberty no longer slumbers,
Error dark no longer cumbers,
  Risen is the sun.
North and south, fell hate defying,
East and west, with love undying,
All in friendship true are vieing,
  Firmly bound in one.
Louder swell the chorus,
Till the welkin o'er us
  Reflects again the joyous strain,
  And discord flies before us.

CHORUS.

Onward press, our country, etc.

H. A. CLARKE.

By permission of Oliver Ditson & Co.
Musical settings are published by them.

Battle Hymn of the Republic.

Key of B♭.   First Note—5.

157

MINE eyes have seen the glory of the coming of the Lord ;
He is trampling out the vintage where the grapes of wrath are stored ;
He hath loosed the fateful lightning of His terrible swift sword,
   His truth is marching on.

CHORUS.

Glory! glory! Hallelujah! Glory! glory! Hallelujah!
Glory! glory! Hallelujah! His truth is marching on.

I have seen Him in the watch-fires of a hundred circling camps ;
They have builded Him an altar in the evening dews and damps ;
I can read His righteous sentence by the dim and flaring lamps,
   His day is marching on.

CHORUS.

Glory! glory! etc.

I have read a fiery gospel, writ in burnished rows of steel ;
"As ye deal with my contemners, so with you my grace shall deal ;
Let the Hero born of woman, crush the serpent with his heel,"
   Since God is marching on.

CHORUS.

Glory! glory! etc.

He has sounded forth the trumpet that shall never
    call retreat ;
He is sifting out the hearts of men before His
    judgment seat ;
Oh, be swift, my soul, to answer Him ! be jubilant,
    my feet !
  Our God is marching on.

CHORUS.

Glory ! glory ! etc.

In the beauty of the lilies, Christ was born across
    the sea,
With a glory in His bosom that transfigures you
    and me ;
As He died to make men holy, let us die to make
    men free,
  While God is marching on.

CHORUS.

Glory ! glory ! etc.

JULIA WARD HOWE.

Long Live America.

Key of B♭   First Note—5.　　　W. H. Pontius.

158

AMERICA, so proud and free,
My song, my heart I give to thee!
Full high thy brave, strong wing has won,
Thine eagle eye is on the sun;
Still upward be thy heav'nward flight,
Still upward mount, till lost in light,
Still upward mount, till lost in light,

CHORUS.

America, so proud and free,
My song, my heart I give to thee;
Long live, long live America!
Long live, long live America!

Thou art so sweet in thy repose,
The world thy friend, abashed thy foes;
Thou seekest not the battle plain,
Thy fields wave with the golden grain;
The sheaves which thou dost garner in,
Come with the harvest's merry din,
Come with the harvest's merry din.

CHORUS.

America, so proud and free, etc.

America, so proud and free,
I give my song, my heart to thee!
Still let thy heav'n-born symbol fly
In every clime, 'neath every sky;
Still rise a yeomen race to stand,
For God and home, and native land.

CHORUS.

America, so proud and free, etc.

　　　　　　　　　　J. E. Rankin, D.D.

By permission of the author.

Cover Them Over with Beautiful Flowers.

Key of E. First Note—5.

159

Cover them over with beautiful flow'rs,
    Deck them with garlands, those brothers of ours,
Lying so silent by night and by day,
Sleeping the years of their manhood away.
Give them the meed they have won in the past;
Give them the honors their future forecast;
Give them the chaplets they won in the strife;
Give them the laurels they lost with their life.

CHORUS.

Cover them over, yes, cover them over,
Parent and husband, brother and lover,
Crown in your hearts those dead heroes of ours,
Cover them over with beautiful flow'rs.

Cover the hearts that have beaten so high,
Beaten with hopes that were doomed but to die;
Hearts that have burned in the heat of the fray;
Hearts that have yearned for the home far away.
Once they were glowing with friendship and love,
Now their great souls have gone soaring above;
Bravely their blood to the nation they gave,
Then in her bosom they found them a grave.

CHORUS.

Cover them over, yes, cover them over,
Parent and husband, brother and lover,
Crown in your hearts those dead heroes of ours,
Cover them over with beautiful flow'rs.

Cover the thousands who sleep far away,
Sleep where their friends cannot find them to-day.
They, who in mountain and hill-side and dell,
Rest where they wearied, and lie where they fell.
Softly the grass-blades creep round their repose;
Sweetly above them the wild flowret blows;
Zephyrs of freedom fly gently o'erhead,
Whispering prayers for the patriot dead.

CHORUS.

Cover them over, yes, cover them over,
Parent and husband, brother and lover,
Crown in your hearts those dead heroes of ours,
Cover them over with beautiful flow'rs.

When the long years have rolled slowly away,
E'en to the dawn of earth's funeral day;
When, at the angel's loud trumpet and tread,
Rise up the faces and forms of the dead.
When the great world its last judgment awaits;
When the blue sky shall fling open its gates,
And our long columns march silently through,
Past the Great Captain for final review.

CHORUS.

Blessings for garlands shall cover them over,
Parent and husband, brother and lover,
God will reward those dead heroes of ours,
Cover them over with beautiful flow'rs.

By permission of Oliver Ditson & Co.
Musical settings are published by them.

The Watch by the Rhine.

Key of C. First Note—1.   Card Wilhelm.

160

A CRY is heard like thunder sound;
   The clash of swords, the waves rebound—
On to the Rhine, our river free!
Who will its brave defenders be?

CHORUS.

Dear Fatherland, may peace be thine!
Dear Fatherland, may peace be thine!
Fast stands and sure the watch, the watch by
   the Rhine,
Fast stands and sure the watch, the watch by
   the Rhine.

A myriad voices join the cry,
A myriad glances flash reply,
Each German, honest, true, and bold,
The sacred boundary will hold!

   Chorus.   Dear Fatherland, etc.

To heav'n his eager glances fly,
Whence heroes gaze approvingly,
And swears, with haughty pride, the Rhine
Shall German be while life is mine!

   Chorus.   Dear Fatherland, etc.

The oath resounds, the stream runs by,
The banners flutter out on high.
On to the Rhine, our river free!
We all will its defenders be!

   Chorus.   Dear Fatherland, etc,

                              MAX SCHENKENBERGER.

Marseilles.

Key of A. First Note—5. Rouget de Lisle.

161

YE sons of France, awake to glory!
  Hark, hark! what myriads bid you rise.
Your children, wives, and grandsires hoary,
  Behold their tears and hear their cries,
  Behold their tears and hear their cries!
Shall hateful tyrants, mischief breeding,
  With hireling hosts, a ruffian band,
  Affright and desolate the land
While peace and liberty lie bleeding?

  To arms, to arms, ye brave!
    Th' avenging sword unsheathe!
  March on, march on! all hearts resolved
    On victory or death!

With luxury and pride surrounded,
  The vile, insatiate despots dare,
Their thirst for gold and pow'r unbounded,
  To mete and vend the light and air.
  To mete and vend the light and air.
Like beasts of burden would they load us,
  Like gods would bid their slaves adore;
But man is man, and who is more?
  Then shall they longer lash and goad us?

Oh, Liberty! can man resign thee,
  Once having felt thy gen'rous flame?
Can dungeons, bolts, and bars confine thee?
  Or whips thy noble spirit tame?
  Or whips thy noble spirit tame?
Too long the world has wept, bewailing,
  That falsehood's dagger tyrants wield;
  But freedom is our sword and shield,
And all their arts are unavailing.

Austrian National Hymn.

Key of F.   First Note—1.   Francis J. Haydn.

162

LAND of greatness! Home of glory!
　　Mighty birthplace of the free;
Famed alike in song and story!
　　All thy sons shall honor thee.
North and South are firmly banded,
　　East and West as one unite!
All by honor well commanded,
　　Strong in striving for the right,
All by honor well commanded,
　　Strong in striving for the right.

2 Noble deeds of old inspiring,
　　Ev'ry heart with lofty aim,
Now our emulation firing,
　　Lead us on to greater fame.
So shall love and truth unshaken,
　　Sturdy courage, honest worth,
Mighty echoes still awaken,
　　To the farthest bounds of earth,
Mighty echoes still awaken,
　　To the farthest bounds of earth.

3 Homes by safe defence surrounded,
　　Rights which make our freedom sure,
Laws on equal justice founded,
　　These will loyalty secure.
While with love and zeal unceasing,
　　We are joining heart and hand,
Shine, in brightness yet increasing,
　　Shine, O dearest Fatherland,
Shine, in brightness yet increasing,
　　Shine, O dearest Fatherland.

　　　　　　　　　　A. J. Foxwell.

Russian National Air.

Key of E. First Note—5.   Alexis Lvoff.

163

God the All-terrible! King, who ordainest
   Great winds Thy clarions, the lightnings
      Thy sword:
Show forth Thy pity on high where Thou
      reignest;
   Give to us peace in our time, O Lord!

2 God the All-merciful! earth hath forsaken
      Thy ways of blessedness, slighted Thy word;
   Bid not Thy wrath in its terrors awaken;
   Give to us peace in our time, O Lord!

3 God the All-righteous One! Man hath defied
      Thee;
   Yet to eternity standeth Thy word;
   Falsehood and wrong shall not tarry beside
      Thee;
   Give to us peace in our time, O Lord!

4 God the All-wise! by the fire of Thy chastening
      Earth shall to freedom and truth be restored;
   Through the thick darkness Thy kingdom is
      hastening;
   Thou wilt give peace in Thy time, O Lord.

Henry F. Chorley.

Index of First Lines.

	HYMN	TUNE
Abide with me : fast falls the eventide	6	Eventide.
A cry is heard like thunder sound	160	Watch by the Rhine.
All hail the power of Jesus' Name	83	Coronation.
All praise to Thee, my God, this night	12	Tallis's Hymn.
America, so proud and free	158	Long Live America.
Am I a soldier of the cross	108	Marlow.
Angels, from the realms of glory	23	Regent Square.
Arm of the Lord, awake ! awake	37	Selwyn.
Art thou weary, art thou languid	55	Stephanos.
At the Lamb's high feast we sing	30	St. George.
Awake, my soul, and with the sun	2	Morning Hymn.
Awake, my soul, stretch every nerve	132	Christmas.
Blessed be the Lord God of Israel	137	Benedictus.
Blest be the tie that binds	126	Boylston.
Blest day of God! most calm, most bright	15	Fernshaw.
Blest of God, the God of Nations	150	Blest of God.
Brightly gleams our banner	113	Vexillum.
Children of the heavenly King	84	Brasted.
Christ the Lord is risen to-day	32	Easter Hymn.
Come, gracious Spirit, heavenly Dove	67	Mendon.
Come, Holy Spirit, heavenly Dove	66	St. Agnes.
Come, praise your Lord and Saviour	117	Ellacombe.
Come, Thou almighty King	71	Moscow.
Come, ye disconsolate, where'er ye languish	124	Come, ye Disconsolate.
Come, ye thankful people, come	26	St. George.
Cover them over with beautiful flowers	159	Beautiful Flowers.
Crown Him with many crowns	64	Diademata.
Eternal Father ! strong to save	44	Melita.
Every morning mercies new	3	Halle.
Father of mercies, bow Thine ear	42	Wareham.
Father of mercies ! in Thy Word	45	Southwell.
Father, whate'er of earthly bliss	120	Naomi.
Fling out the banner! let it float	34	Camden.
Forward ! be our watchword	116	Warfare.
From every stormy wind that blows	96	Retreat.
From glory unto glory	27	Berthold.
From Greenland's icy mountains	35	Missionary Hymn.

	HYMN	TUNE
From the hillside, from the hollow	156	March of the Men of Columbia.
Glorious things of thee are spoken	102	Glorious Things.
Glory be to God on high	136	Gloria in Excelsis.
God be merciful unto us	142	Deus Misereatur.
God the all-terrible, King	163	Russian National Air.
Gracious God, our Heavenly Father	1	Regent Square.
Guide me, O Thou great Jehovah	77	Autumn.
Hail, Columbia! happy land	153	Hail, Columbia.
Hail to the brightness of Zion's glad morning	69	Wesley.
Hail to the Lord's anointed	90	Webb.
Hark, hark, my soul	73	Pilgrims.
Hark! the herald angels sing	18	Herald Angels.
He leadeth me! oh, blessed thought	122	Aughton.
Holy, Holy, Holy, Lord God Almighty	68	Nicæa.
How firm a foundation, ye saints of the Lord	123	Adeste Fideles.
I heard the voice of Jesus say	91	Vox Dilecti.
I love Thy kingdom, Lord	98	St. Thomas.
I need Thee every hour	95	Need.
In loud exalted strains	97	King of Glory.
Inspirer and hearer of prayer	125	Protection.
In the cross of Christ I glory	61	Rathburn.
In the hour of trial	54	Penitence.
It came upon the midnight clear	20	Carol.
It is a good thing to give thanks	141	Bonum est Confiteri.
I will lift up mine eyes unto the hills	147	
I would not live alway	93	Frederick.
Jerusalem, the golden	75	Urbs Beata.
Jesu, lover of my soul	51	Refuge.
Jesus Christ is risen to-day	29	Easter Hymn.
Jesus shall reign where'er the sun	36	Duke Street.
Jesus, Thy name I love	118	Lyte.
Joy to the world! the Lord is come	24	Nativity.
Just as I am, without one plea	121	St. Crispin.
Lamp of our feet, whereby we trace	50	St. Peter.
Land of greatness! Home of glory	162	Austrian National Hymn.
Lead, kindly Light, amid the encircling gloom	79	Lux Benigna.
Lead us, heavenly Father, lead us	78	Dulce Carmen.
Lift up your heads, ye mighty gates	85	Sefton.
Lord, dismiss us with Thy blessing	134	Greenville.
Lord of all being; throned afar	46	Mendon.
Lord, when we bend before Thy throne	59	Martyrdom.
Love divine, all love excelling	80	Love Divine
Mine eyes have seen the glory	157	Battle Hymn of the Republic.

	HYMN	TUNE
More love to Thee, O Christ	133	More Love.
My country! 'tis of thee	151	America.
My faith looks up to Thee	57	Olivet.
My God, permit me not to be	58	Hamburg.
My soul doth magnify the Lord	139	Magnificat.
Nearer, my God, to Thee	56	Bethany.
Now from the altar of our hearts	13	Belmont.
Now the day is over	8	Merrial.
O be joyful in the Lord	138	Jubilate Deo.
O could I speak the matchless worth	131	Ariel.
O day of rest and gladness	16	Dies Dominica.
O happy band of pilgrims	110	Lincoln.
O Jesu, Thou art standing	60	St. Edith.
O Lamb of God, still keep me	62	Jesu, Magister Bone.
O little town of Bethlehem	22	St. Louis.
O Lord of hosts, Whose glory fills	43	Wareham.
O Lord, our strength in weakness	48	Conquest.
O Mother dear, Jerusalem	74	Materna.
O Paradise, O Paradise	72	Paradise.
O praise the Lord, for it is a good thing	144	
O Saviour, precious Saviour	82	Watermouth.
O sing unto the Lord	140	Cantate Domino
O Thou through suffering perfect made	39	Intercession.
O Thou, Who madest land and sea	40	Melita.
Oh, bless the Lord, my soul	92	St. Thomas.
Oh, Columbia, the gem of the ocean	154	Red, White, and Blue.
Oh come, all ye faithful	17	Adeste Fideles.
Oh, help us, Lord; each hour of need	53	St. Peter.
Oh, say, can you see	152	Star Spangled Banner.
Oh, where shall rest be found	112	Dennis.
Oh, worship the King, all glorious above	88	Hanover.
Once more, my soul, the rising day	4	Warwick.
One sweetly solemn thought	128	Dawn.
Onward, Christian soldiers	114	St. Gertrude.
Our blest Redeemer, ere He breathed	65	St. Cuthbert.
Our Father, who art in heaven	149	
Pass me not, O gentle Saviour	47	Pass Me Not.
Pleasant are Thy courts above	101	St. George, or Windsor.
Praise, my soul, the King of heaven	87	Dulce Carmen.
Praise the Lord, O my soul	143	Benedic Anima Mea.
Praise to God, immortal praise	25	Dix.
Prayer is the soul's sincere desire	106	Byefield.
Rejoice, the Lord is King	86	Rejoice.
Rise, crowned with light, imperial Salem	99	Russian Hymn.
Rise, my soul, and stretch thy wings	111	Beethoven.
Rock of ages, cleft for me	52	Toplady.

Hymn		Tune
Round the Lord in glory seated	70	Moultrie.
Saviour, again to Thy dear Name we raise	14	Ellerton.
Saviour, blessed Saviour	115	David.
Saviour, I follow on	105	Eden.
Saviour, source of every blessing	81	Trust.
Shine on our souls, eternal God	9	Chesterfield.
Shout the glad tidings, exultingly sing	21	Avesion.
Softly now the light of day	11	Weber.
Soldiers of Christ, arise	109	Diademata.
Songs of praise the angels sang	94	Vienna.
Stand up, stand up, for Jesus	119	Webb.
Sun of my soul, Thou Saviour dear	10	Hursley.
The breaking waves dashed high	155	Breaking [Waves.
The Church's one foundation	103	Aurelia.
The day of resurrection	31	Rotterdam.
The earth is the Lord's	145	Domini est Terra.
The heavens declare the glory of God	148	
The King of love my Shepherd is	76	Dominus Regit Me.
The Lord is my Shepherd, how happy am I	5	Forsaken.
The Lord is my Shepherd I shall not want	146	Dominus Regit Me.
The morning light is breaking	33	Webb.
The shadows of the evening hours	7	St. Leonard.
The Son of God goes forth to war	107	All Saints.
The spacious firmament on high	89	Creation.
There is a blessèd home	127	Blessed Home.
Thou art gone up on high	63	St. Barnabas.
Thou Who with dying lips	41	Broadlands.
Triumphant Sion, lift thy head	100	Wareham.
		[Windsor.
Watchman, tell us of the night	49	St. George, or
We give Thee but Thine own	38	Cambridge.
We praise Thee, O God	135	Te Deum.
While shepherds watched their flocks	19	Gabriel.
While Thee I seek, protecting Power	129	Spohr.
While with ceaseless course the sun	28	Benevento.
Work, for the night is coming	104	Work Song.
Worship the Lord in the beauty of holiness	130	Salamis.
Ye sons of France, awake to glory	161	Marseilles.

www.ingramcontent.com/pod-product-compliance
Lightning Source LLC
Chambersburg PA
CBHW032147160426
43197CB00008B/810